PAWS IN THE PROCEEDINGS

Just over a year ago, Deric enjoyed intermittent visits from a black feral tomcat called Eric, who used the cellar as a refuge from the wife and kids. One day Eric disappeared, but the *Huddersfield Examiner* reported that the RSPCA had captured a pair of feral cats and three of their kittens – a fourth had escaped. Next morning, in Deric's garden, was a half-grown kitten, black as coal – which is how Nokia joined Deric, his wife Aileen and their two ageing cats, Tigger and Thermal, and enjoyed the adventures which come from sharing your home with a troop of small cats with big personalities!

PAWS IN THE PROCEEDINGS

PAWS IN THE PROCEEDINGS

by

Deric Longden

Magna Large Print Books
Long Preston, North Yorkshire,
BD23 4ND, England.

British Library Cataloguing in Publication Data.

Longden, Deric
    Paws in the proceedings.

    A catalogue record of this book is
    available from the British Library

    ISBN   978-0-7505-2841-2

First published in Great Britain in 2007 by Bantam Press

Published in Large Print 2008 by arrangement with
Transworld Publishers

Magna Large Print is an imprint of Library Magna Books Ltd.

Printed and bound in Great Britain by
T.J. (International) Ltd., Cornwall, PL28 8RW

CHAPTER ONE

They didn't have any of those lightweight racing trolleys jacked up on the starting blocks outside Sainsbury's, just a regular army of the extra-outsize models that have been specially designed to take four dozen cans of Guinness, a small wardrobe, and a three-piece suite. So I settled for a basket instead.

And then I couldn't remember for the life of me what I was supposed to be putting into it. I had made a list and I knew exactly where it was: on the kitchen table at home.

Just inside the shop doorway I turned to a woman who was staring into space by the cut flowers and bedding plants.

'Have you any idea what I've come in for?'

She hadn't, apparently, and she was mightily relieved to be steered away by an older woman who arrived clutching twenty Silk Cut and a copy of the *Huddersfield Examiner*.

'What did he want?'

'I've no idea, Mother – I think he's a bit simple.'

On balance I tended to agree with her and minutes later I was standing in front of a rather fetching display of assorted cat litter. One thing I can guarantee is that I certainly came in for cat litter. It's always there at the top of the shopping list along with lottery ticket, garlic sausage for Tigger and two green bananas for Aileen.

One of the lousiest jobs in a supermarket must be having to arrange the display of cat litter.

'And make it look interesting.'

They'd tried. Each pair of hernia-inducing bags had been interspersed with a can of cat-litter spray and a packet of worming powder, and right in the middle of this fascinating arrangement stood a triangular Perspex box containing a chicken and oak-smoked ham sandwich in wholemeal bread, though on second thoughts I think that must have been planted there by a customer who had gone over budget.

I squatted and sat back on my knees in order to examine the cat litter. I had never noticed before that Sainsbury's stock two different lines, 'clumping' and 'non-clumping'. To clump or not to clump – that was the question.

I'm beginning to think aloud these days. It comes along with the grey hairs and the afternoon naps and is an integral part of the 'Now what the hell have I come upstairs for?' syndrome.

A lady arrived by my side, towering above

me as I knelt. She had a very sexy voice and a beautifully turned pair of ankles to match.

'I always buy the clumping cat litter for our Alan.'

I eased my head slightly to the right and addressed her rather sexy left knee.

'I can't remember which I have.'

As her left knee kindly pointed out to me the many advantages that the clumping cat litter has over the non-clumping variety, my mind had a good stretch and then went walkabout. I couldn't help wondering about our Alan. He couldn't be her cat, could he?

Alan isn't a cat's name. In my time I have been the proud servant of a veritable battalion of cats, the noble Arthur and the dopey William amongst them. I have been closely associated with an ancient roll of clingfilm called Colin, a mild-mannered sultana by the name of Ralph and a heat-seeking missile, a feral known as Eric, who until recently was holed up by the boiler in the cellar, mostly fast asleep on Aileen's Pilates workout machine.

But the name Alan doesn't work for a cat. It doesn't cross over. It's a two-legged name, just as you can be sure that anything called Fido will most certainly have four legs, a waggy tail and bad breath.

As I wandered through the store with my hundredweight of clumping cat litter slung over my shoulder, quietly thanking God that it hadn't been one of this week's 'buy three for the price of two' offers, I stopped for a rest at the delicatessen, and there, buying three slices of ham off the bone, was Alan's lovely owner, or possibly mother.

I waited – I had to know. Alan could just conceivably be her husband. Maybe he was having a bit of trouble with his waterworks and the cat litter was part of an innovative and well thought out plan to ease him on his way towards the lavatory. Hardly likely, but possible.

As I stood there my eyes were drawn to a small sign that had been rammed deep into an innocent sausage roll. *Free-Range Pork Pies*.

Instantly my mind was off once more, this time to a sunny knoll atop a flower-sprinkled meadow somewhere deep in the heart of the English countryside where a couple of rather mature Melton Mowbrays were keeping a watchful eye on their little individual pork pies as they romped gaily amongst the buttercups and daisies below.

'Your Alan's getting to be a big lad – isn't he?'
'Aye – and he can be a little bugger at times.'

Now they had been roped and tied and placed under glass, and it had just struck me that Alan isn't a bad name for an individual pork pie when a voice brought me racing back into what passes for the real world.

'Hello again.'

'Hi.'

We walked together past the milk products and on through the red wine and canned beer towards the tills, leaving behind us a crunchy trail of clumping cat litter.

'I've been worrying about your Alan.'

'How come?'

'It just seems a strange name for a cat.'

She insisted that I go first since I only had the one item. I thanked her and rammed my item into two carrier bags in order to stop the leak and then had to take it out again so that the cashier could read the bar code.

'Do you think so? I've never thought about it. There were two of them at first. Two little kittens, both boys. We had them for about a year or so and they were really good pals and then poor little Flanagan got run over by a bus.'

I was glad I had persisted. It all made sense now and my mind was able to take a few minutes off, curled up in its favourite corner of my head. Round at the back where it can't see out.✗

Flanagan and Allen. When I was a kid I had a matching pair of baby rabbits called Laurel and Hardy. My mother painted their names on the front of the hutch. She had suggested we call them Rawicz and Landauer after a couple of pianists who were all the rage on the wireless at the time, but in the end she decided that neither of the rabbits looked quite Jewish enough and anyway she couldn't spell Rawicz – or Landauer for that matter.

As I turned the car into Park Drive I began to rehearse my excuses for having forgotten Tigger's garlic sausage. She has to be careful what she eats these days. She only has the one tooth left now and she's very embarrassed about it. She doesn't smile as readily as she used to and her snores have taken on a high-pitched whistle which can be rather intrusive when Thermal and I are trying to watch football on television. It's also slightly off-putting for the referee who keeps glancing around him to see who else is getting in on the act.

I have nothing against Tigger's tooth, but then neither has Tigger and so pâtés are the order of the day, along with finely chopped tuna, corned beef and her weekly packet of garlic sausage.

She was sitting on top of the stone gatepost when I arrived, having her nose rubbed by our new neighbour Aileen Ireland. I don't know, you wait forty-odd years for an Aileen to come into your life and then two come along at once – it's always the same, isn't it?

She had brought me a present from the Farmers' Market in Holmfirth and was let-

12

ting Tigger have a sniff at the packet.

'It's sheep's cheese – there's not a lot of it, but it was rather pricey. I asked the farmer why it cost so much.'

'What did he say?'

'He asked me if I'd ever tried milking a sheep.'

Tigger is showing her age these days. I offered to help her down from the gatepost but she insisted on doing it her own way. At one time this would have involved a gazelle-like leap that gracefully cleared the considerable spread of the flowering privet before an elegant switch into slow motion parachute mode, during which she would hover in mid-air whilst calmly deciding which of the paving stones would make for the softest landing.

But today she dithered, this way and that. Dare she tiptoe across the narrow top of the wrought iron gate and down onto the lower wall over on the other side? How about a controlled slide down the sheer face of the huge stone gatepost? Her crampons are not what they used to be and the arthritis in her hips shivered at the thought.

'Let me give you a hand.'

'I'm not helpless.'

'Suit yourself.'

As I dragged the cat litter out of the boot I wondered how she had got up there in the first place. Probably the paper boy. His little dog can't be doing with cats and insists that the paper boy go up the path first so that he can pick up any offending moggie that might be mooching around and place it well out of the way, on a window sill, up a tree or on a gatepost.

She was still up there, trying to work it out, as I staggered past with the cat litter. Thermal was in the walled garden, crouched on a railway sleeper, half hidden amongst the lower branches of a fir tree and surrounded by ivy
   'Shhh.'
   I shushed and sat down beside him. High up on the wall a blue tit's bum was sticking out of a small gap between the stones. His mate was perched on the hanging basket immediately below.
   They'd been back time and time again over the past week to have a look at this most desirable site, but it was never going to be large enough for a growing family. Which was why I had been hard at work up a ladder, chipping away at the mortar and hauling out loose rubble from the back. I had thought of a carpet and a fitted kitchen but there hadn't been time.
   My motives were entirely selfish. If they moved in I would be able sit at the breakfast table and watch them as they went about

their daily routine.

The little blue bum swivelled and a little blue face appeared.

'I must admit, Maureen – it's bigger than I thought it was.'

This was just what Maureen wanted to hear and they swopped places so that she could have a look round and measure up for curtains. She was out again in no time and joined him excitedly on the hanging basket below.

'It's perfect, Maurice – and you always wanted a garden.'

And then they were off across the park, probably to check out the local schools.

I left Thermal to keep an eye on the bag of cat litter and went to check on Tigger. She'd settled back down on the gatepost, squatting as a mother hen would, covering her chickens.

'Help.'

Someone once said that dogs come when you call, but cats take a message and then get back to you.

Even so, she would panic if I made a grab for her and so I just stood there by the towering gatepost giving her time to work it out for herself. After a few moments a paw reached out and planted itself on the top of my head, another joining it as soon as Tigger thought it safe, buttoning itself up tightly to the first. Then a rear paw decided to get in on the act and in no time at all I had a small tortoiseshell cat sitting on the top of my head.

We have tried this before and it usually works very well. The next move is for me to ease myself down three or four steps until I am just inside the front gate; then, slowly, keeping my upper body absolutely still so that she feels perfectly secure, I lower myself until I am sitting on the bottom step. Tigger can then walk off my head onto the top of the low wall, at the end of which she only has a six-inch jump down onto the paving stones.

Only this time she stayed put. She's seventeen years old now and likes to think things over, so she decided to have a good wash first.

I was saying to Aileen only the other day: 'Tigger doesn't seem to wash herself any more.'

Aileen thought about it for a moment.

'She probably has someone in.'

Tigger took her time and gave herself a really good going-over, paying special attention to her white bits and her split ends. She seemed to have relaxed somewhat, and as her claws were no longer stapling her to my scalp I comforted myself with the thought that all this was probably very good for my posture.

16

We must have sat there for some time. A different take on togetherness, with Tigger fettling away like mad and me having beautiful thoughts about nothing in particular. I have a lot of those. Often they are in colour. Magenta is my favourite, with tangerine running it a close second, and one day a man in a white coat is going to sit me down and explain them to me.

We were each deep in our different worlds when a woman's voice cut through our respective reveries.

'I've only come out 'cos I'm mad wi' my dog.'

I turned my head, rather like the gun turret on a Sherman tank, slowly so as not to unsettle Tigger and together we surveyed the tiny wisp of a woman who was addressing us through the wrought iron bars of the gate.

I have come across her several times and I still have no idea who she is. She's never after a deep meaningful conversation. She makes a statement, repeats it and then buzzes off across the park, and she'll only talk at all if there is a barrier between us, such as the gate.

On the last occasion she caught me up a ladder, painting the garage.

'I haven't been in our front room for weeks. My husband's got a plant in there what eats flies and it turns my stomach.'

Tigger had turned round so that she now had her back to the woman and I had her miserable excuse for a tail hanging down between my eyes.

'I've only come out 'cos I'm mad wi' my dog.'

Not for one moment did she seem to find it strange that she was talking to a Davy Crockett lookalike with his hat on back to front – not even when the hat casually hopped off his head and had a great big stretch on the lower wall.

I wanted to ask her about her dog and the terrible deed that had driven her out of the house. I could imagine her slamming the front door: 'And I want all that cleaned up by the time I get back.'

But deep down I knew that she didn't have a dog, or a husband – maybe not even a front door. She only ever appears when the white van is parked across the road. The white van with its fragile cargo of a dozen or so poor lost souls and their four or five minders who have all on keeping their charges in a straight line as they work their way round the park. It isn't easy when most of them take two steps sideways for every one forwards. Especially when the miniature railway is up and running and the excitement reaches fever pitch.

I stood up to have a word with her, but she was off across to the park, pausing only to look right and then left and then right again, like a three-year-old who had learned the Green Cross code only that morning.

A burly young man was waiting to escort her. He put his arm round her and in no time at all she was folded back into the crocodile of the walking wounded.

Feeling quite light-headed now that my hat had taken its leave I turned to climb the steps. Tigger was still sitting on the low wall.

'Come on.'

She rose stiffly to her feet and contemplated the six-inch drop down onto the path. Then she sat down again and looked at me with her big green eyes, so I picked her up, tucked her under my arm and set off towards the front door.

With winter on its way her arthritis is going to go from bad to worse. She sets like concrete in the winter. I wonder if I ought to have her lagged.

CHAPTER TWO

Aileen sat at the kitchen table with her back to the window. The sunlight confuses her and she is confused enough by the outside world as it is.

She stirred her coffee absently – I had watched her stir her coffee a dozen times in the last five minutes as she gazed into the distance.

'What are you thinking about?'

This time she stirred herself and came back from wherever it was she had been. 'I was just wondering if I should teach you how to resuscitate me if ever I choke.'

You have to think on your feet with Aileen.

'Tomorrow,' I said. 'You won't be choking before then, will you?'

'Probably not.'

'What about the crossword instead?'

We do the cryptic crossword in the *Daily Telegraph* every day. It's very much a fifty-fifty effort. I read out a clue to my beautiful blind wife in a clear distinct voice. She tells me the answer in a matter of seconds and I write it in very neatly. Unless it's a down clue. I can't spell downhill and she has to talk me through it. Teamwork or what?

We zipped through the first half a dozen in no time at all and then I bowled her a bouncer.

'Fourteen letters – nothing in it.'

She has trouble with overlong anagrams. 'The letters won't keep still in my head.'

We decided to leave that one until we had a few odd letters threaded through it. They act as stabilizers and then she's off and running.

'Four letters – Beheaded crowbar wins critics' award.'

She smiled at me. Well, not at me exactly – she smiled at where I would have been if I hadn't got up to pour us each a second cup of coffee.

'You should know that one.'

I must admit that I'm much more at home with four letter words – five letters and I'm getting a bit out of my depth.

'Give me a clue.'

'What sort of crowbar do burglars use?'

'A jemmy?'

'Chop its head off.'

It doesn't take long for me to catch on.

'An Emmy.'

I should have had that straight away – we have an Emmy upstairs. It's on the sideboard, standing in between our two offices, tucked away from the general thoroughfare of the house because it wouldn't do for anyone to think we were showing off.

I suppose that's a very British thing to do. If I were a Hollywood actor I would have it floodlit in a glass case by the front door. But this is Huddersfield and we don't do things like that. Anyway, somebody might nick it.

I had been on a book-signing tour when I heard that my television play *Lost For Words* had been nominated for an International Emmy award in New York.

It had been one of those tortuous book tours that seem to have been organized with the help of a road map of Lithuania. First day in Manchester, then off down south and left a bit to Norwich, then straight back up country and across to Liverpool. The next port of call was to be Eastbourne, nice place but a long way away, and my car had already developed a nervous twitch and a pronounced limp.

So when the executive producer Keith Richardson rang from Yorkshire Television to tell me the good news and asked if I would be free to go to New York for the ceremony I thought sod Eastbourne, and almost before I knew it I was pushing Thora Hird's wheelchair round the streets of the Big Apple.

I had taken Thora out many times before. She stayed at the Huddersfield Hotel whenever she filmed a series of *Last of the Summer Wine* and was always eager to take a trip down to the open market, where she thought the toilet rolls and kitchen rolls were remarkable value.

The only problem was getting her down there and back in the same day. Everyone in the country recognized Thora Hird and we would have gone about ten yards before someone would stare in disbelief, then stop her.

'It is – isn't it?'

They would ease themselves down to wheelchair height and chat, as to an old friend. Which of course in a way she was. She gave good value for money, swapping story for story until she took over the conversation completely. I would stand there, like one of those dogs in the park whose owners know everyone. Except that I couldn't pass the time by sticking my back leg in the air and licking my bum.

Then off we would go again, for another ten yards.

'It is – isn't it?'

It could take hours, but the journey back to the hotel was always that bit quicker – simply because she was harder to spot, surrounded by a solid wall of cheap toilet rolls and kitchen rolls.

She enjoyed the recognition because everyone genuinely loved her, but here in New York it was a very different story. No one knew who the hell she was and it must have been very strange for her in these crowded streets, at the age of eighty-eight, an established leading lady playing the part of an extra – an anonymous old lady in a wheelchair.

That night we attended the Emmys ceremony at the Hilton in just about the largest ballroom I have ever seen in my life. We were on table five hundred and fifty-one, which seemed to be situated roughly five miles south of the Mason-Dixon line.

Thora was very tired and the night seemed to go on for ever, but like the trouper she was she stuck it out until the end of the evening when the award for the most outstanding drama programme was to be presented.

Pete Postlethwaite couldn't be there as he was filming in Canada, but we had been joined by Thora's lovely daughter Janette Scott-Rademaekers and our director Alan J.W. Bell and his wife, and we all held our breath as Peter Ustinov showed clips of the four nominated films and then, with great deliberation, opened the envelope and read out the result.

'The winner is *Lost For Words.*'

A few years ago *Wide-Eyed and Legless* had been nominated for a BAFTA and lost by a short lead. 'Well, it's enough just to be here.' The hell it is. There really is nothing like winning, and we were up on that gigantic stage like a shot – men, women and wheel-chair.

We all made speeches and none of us had any idea what we were going to say and still have no idea of what we said. We had a party afterwards and the champagne flowed as champagne has a habit of doing on these occasions until well after three o'clock in the morning, when we thought it safe to ring the kids back at home as they were getting ready for work.

The next day Keith Richardson took us all out to lunch at the Algonquin. I couldn't wait. It was more than forty years since I first promised myself that one day I would sit in the dining room there, at the famous round table.

Back in the 1950s I was reluctantly inching my way through a couple of years of National Service in the RAF at Hereford when I was set to work for the adjutant, a Flight Lieu-tenant Cassell. He was a member of the Cassell's publishing family and he must have seen something in me because he began to force feed me from the cases of books which always seemed to surround him.

At home we only had the one book. My father won a Sunday school competition when he was a kid and his prize was a copy of *Mr Midshipman Easy*. It had never been opened in all those years and after he died I discovered that several of the pages were still uncut at the top.

At Hereford I devoured three or four books a week and then one day I read a piece by Robert Benchley and loved his gentle humour. In it he mentioned the writer Dorothy Parker and I searched for ages and eventually found her kicking her heels, unloved and unwanted, in one of the stockrooms at Hereford library.

I was immediately caught by her more abrasive style. In one of her bittersweet pieces she mentioned Alexander Woollcott, George S. Kaufman and the Algonquin round table and I was off and running. I read them all.

In the late 1920s all these writers and more lunched regularly at the legendary round table in the Algonquin hotel, where the conversation sparkled and the wit flowed like wine and they were greeted at the door by a tortoiseshell cat called Rusty.

I didn't expect Rusty to be there to greet me. He'd be well over eighty by now and long retired with his pipe and his slippers to a condominium in New Hampshire.

But as we pushed open the door of the hotel and spilled into the foyer, there, stretched out on a silver tray and surrounded by ivy, was a most elegant and beautiful white cat. He rose as we approached and purred as I stroked him and said how pleased he was to

26

see us and hoped we would enjoy our meal.

I couldn't have hoped for a more perfect welcome, and there was more to come. I sat myself down at the round table and above the fireplace there was a painting of my literary heroes and heroines seated at the very same table, as though I were looking into a mirror and they had all joined me for lunch. I told them I had just won an Emmy and they were thrilled for me.

And then it was time to get back to England. We were waiting for a taxi in the hotel foyer when a thought crossed Thora's mind. Whenever she flew anywhere from Heathrow it didn't matter what sort of ticket she bought. She was always upgraded to first class as soon as she approached the ticket desk.

'It is – isn't it?'

But out in the streets of New York nobody had recognized her. She turned to Janette.

'Where's my Emmy?'

'I've packed it.'

'Well unpack it. I'm having it on my knee.'

At Kennedy airport the girl behind the desk squealed with delight as she caught sight of the gold statuette.

'My God – is that an Emmy? Come this way.'

And the hostess whipped them off to the

27

first class lounge. Aileen and I were next in line and I flashed the girl one of my famous winning smiles.

'I've got one as well.'

She flashed me one of those infamous smiles that are reserved solely for the use of those who have to deal with people like me, day in, day out.

'I'm sure you have, sir.'

And when we reached the plane Thora turned left for the champagne and the neck massage and Aileen and I turned right.

Some things never change.

From New York to London and then on to Leeds Bradford airport. We touched down at around lunchtime and on the way home called in at the ITV television studios in Leeds where they had a huge banner stretched across the front of the building in honour of our producer Keith Richardson.

WELCOME TO OUR TARTAN LEADER.

More champagne and congratulations and then home to Huddersfield and two very indignant cats. They cut us dead.

'*How could you leave us like that?*'

'*Don't talk to him, Thermal – he's not worth it.*'

Aileen polished off the final two clues in no time at all and we had another crossword done and dusted.

'That was brilliant, love. You're fantastic.'

'Thank you.'

'I'm rubbish.'

'No you're not.'

She can be very kind. She doesn't like to see my ego dragging itself along the carpet and she does her level best to lift it skywards.

'You're just very average.'

We had been lucky to get through a whole lunch and a crossword without being interrupted by our duo of feline foragers, but now there were sounds of stirring fur in the dining area. Both Thermal and Tigger sleep in there and when I say sleep we are talking about twenty-one hours in the average day.

We have bought each of them one of those small oil-filled radiators that come up to just below my knee, but which are head high to the average cat. The radiators provide a top to toe roasting and in front of each one there is a very small sheepskin rug, stylishly fashioned from a very small sheep.

The cats always arrive at the kitchen table buttoned up together like Siamese twins, but once under cover of the table they separate, Thermal banging his flank hard against Aileen's ankle, Tigger against mine.

'*We're here.*'

And then, rejoined at the hip, they sit staring intently at the fridge door, believing that through the power of their joint person-alities they can persuade the door to swing wide open.

The fact that this has never actually hap-pened in the last sixteen years hasn't served to dull their belief, but then their rumbling stomachs tell them that there is always a next time and they decide to cut corners by standing on their hind legs and clawing their way in through the door.

'No.'

This order, barked out by the fearsome man of the house, is always obeyed imme-diately and they stop short and sit and stare again in unison until Tigger, who simply can't bear to be told what to do, raises one limp paw and with her claws completely withdrawn taps gently just once against the door.

'I'm not having him talking to me like that.'
'You do right.'

CHAPTER THREE

Three and a half hours after arriving home from New York I was in the car and tootling down the M1 towards Waterstone's book-shop in Nottingham wondering how on earth I was supposed to switch the sidelights on.

I remember coming to the conclusion that I was probably jetlagged. I'd had the car for all of three years now and I was sure I must have switched the lights on at some time or other during that period, but every time I tweaked a likely-looking knob, either the radio burst into life or I washed the wind-screen.

Richard Weaver who represents Transworld Publishers in that neck of the woods was waiting for me when I finally found the bookshop. He was chatting to Mick Peat, who arranges my talks around these parts, and between them they eased me through the next few hours. Mick reminded me what my name was whenever I was about to sign a book and Richard slapped a fresh copy in front of me on those occasions when I signed it to Doris instead of Sandra. The audience was very kind and somehow I got through the evening all in one piece.

It was getting on for midnight and I was on the way home when I tried to phone Aileen. She had curled up on the settee and fallen fast asleep the moment we had arrived home from the States and she was still out to the wide as I set off on my journey down to Nottingham.

I only ever use my mobile phone to keep in touch with Aileen, to talk her through the contents of the fridge or just sort out the kind of problem that occurs on a regular basis when the world in front of you is nothing more than a shadowland of strange and possibly hostile obstacles.

My mobile is hands-free. It sits in a neat little cradle attached to the dashboard and a microphone is tucked up in the top of the door. All I have to do is press number one and wait until Aileen eventually finds the phone at the other end, and we have lift-off.

The only problem is that, recently, on each occasion when I have pressed number one, for some reason I have spoken to the very nice Pakistani gentleman who runs the Asian takeaway in Marsh.

I decided to give it a shot anyway. Thankfully I am made of stern stuff and was able to resist the temptation of today's special offer: pay for one chicken tikka masala, get one free.

So I pulled the car over and tried to ring Aileen in the old-fashioned way as God had intended. The only problem was that for the life of me I couldn't remember our telephone number. Not even the area code.

For once I had a bright idea – it's not something that happens to me all that often and it cheered me up immensely. I had searched through my wallet for one of my business cards in order to find my phone number, but discovered that I had given them all away. So I rang directory enquiries and gave my home address to a pleasant young lady who would tell me my telephone number in no time at all.

'I'm sorry – it's ex-directory.'

'But it's me.'

'I'm sorry.'

'It's my telephone number.'

'Sorry, sir.'

And that was that. Still, I don't suppose they can hand out unlisted numbers at will just because the caller happens to tell them that it's him.

Then bright idea number two tapped me on the shoulder. As I searched through my wallet I had noticed one of my son Nick's business cards tucked up in a handy compartment. Nick was planning to open a second restaurant, this time in Nice on the French Riviera, and he was over there now.

So from Nottingham in the East Midlands I rang Nick in the South of France to ask him for my own telephone number in deepest West Yorkshire.

'Oh my God, Dad, what are we going to do with you?'

I tried to explain as best I could. After all, it seemed to make some kind of sense to me.

'Never mind, Dad. Lisa and I will be back next week and then we'll find you a nice little place. Somewhere where you can have your own room and they'll look after you properly.'

He can be a sarcastic little devil.

I rang the number he gave me. I had a feeling I'd seen it somewhere before. It was engaged, so I decided to give it a few moments before I tried again, and pulled back into the traffic.

I had driven through the centre of Nottingham and was on my way out towards the motorway when my phone burst into life. It had to be Aileen, it always was.

'Hello, darling.'

Richard Weaver's unmistakably masculine tones rang out. He'd followed me in his car all the way through the town from Waterstone's.

'Hello, sweetheart. Switch your bloody lights on.'

I seem to have come to an emergency stop

as far as modern technology is concerned. My brain is full up. It's stuck in the past, still wearing flared trousers and winklepickers.

When I moved up a notch from the video recorder it took me a month to come to terms with the new DVD player, and by that time I had completely forgotten how to use the fax machine. It's as though whenever something fresh needs to go into my head, then something else has to move out to make room for it.

I have friends who can pick up a stranger's mobile phone and within minutes be taking photographs with it. On the other hand, I have friends who make me feel almost normal.

A little while ago I drove over to Hyde, just outside Manchester, to see Tony Husband. He is the brilliant cartoonist who created the Yobs for *Private Eye* magazine and his funny little men with their overblown noses are to be seen everywhere.

He had popped out to post some letters and on his way back he called in at the newsagent's. He was sorting out his change when he realized that he still had the bunch of envelopes in his hand.

'Oh my God – I've posted my mobile.'

He waited ages for the postman to come and empty the box. He had heard that once an item enters the system it becomes the property of Her Majesty and it takes a hell of a long time before it can be returned. So when the postman eventually came round the corner Tony went down on bended knees. He couldn't manage without it, he pleaded. He would miss so many calls, and in his line of business time was of the essence.

'Please – just this one time.'

The postman seemed completely oblivious of his presence and coolly went about shovelling the contents of the postbox into his sack. Then he came across the mobile phone and plonked it into Tony's hand.

'There you are.'

And he was gone, leaving Tony down on the pavement, doing his world-famous impression of Toulouse-Lautrec.

At least he knows how to use his mobile phone. I am more in tune with my old friend Margaret Bramley when it comes to dealing with the mysteries of the modern world.

For years she lived in a flat just down the road from me. High up in my office window, through the steam of my morning coffee, I would watch her as she took the elderly and arthritic Alfred out for his daily walk in Greenhead Park.

Alfred was a fine old dog. He was patience personified. He would sigh and cock his leg as best he could, and then sit down and lick his bum in resignation as Margaret stopped to have yet another ten-minute conversation with an old friend, or perhaps with someone she had never even met before in her life.

It would take them all morning to work their way round the park. By the time they eventually made their way home Alfred's bum would be a credit to him, clean as a new whistle and gleaming in the morning sunlight. When Alfred sadly passed away Margaret decided that was that – no more dogs.

Then Nellie came along. Nellie had led a troubled life and had perfected obstinacy down to a fine art. If she decided she'd had enough she would lie on her back with all of her four legs up in the air.

But Nellie had met her match in Margaret Bramley. Margaret would drag the supine animal round the park, over the pavement edge and across the road, until Nellie conceded there must be more to life than this.

She turned into a lovely little dog. The sort of dog you could take home to meet your mother. But then Margaret, who was beginning to find the day-to-day business of life increasingly difficult, had to go into sheltered housing and the two of them ceased to be part of my daily routine.

In the flesh, that is. I began to receive a series of telephone calls – as many as a dozen or so in half an hour. There was never anyone on the other end. Every now and then I thought I could hear grunting, maybe in frustration, and then there would be silence for an hour or so until the pantomime was played out all over again.

I was getting really annoyed with these constant interruptions, and then one day I picked up the phone and heard a voice shouting in the distance.

'Bugger!'

I knew that voice – but I just couldn't place it.

'Don't do that, Nellie. You'll have it over.'

I rang Margaret's son and he said he would look into it. A little later he rang me back with the problem all done and dusted.

He had set his mother up in her new home with a brand new television set and a mobile phone which she could take around with her. That way she would never be out of touch. In order that she would find the phone easy to operate she only had to press the number one button to get her son at home, or number two to ring his brother's house. I had the privilege of being programmed in at number three.

Unfortunately the state of the art television set had a remote control unit. She had never come across one of those before and in her confusion every now and then she would try to change channels with the mobile phone. Her favourite channel was ITV, which was where my number three came into the story – a dozen times or so in half an hour. Her son apologized for the inconvenience but he didn't need to – I understood perfectly.

I arrived back from Nottingham in the early hours. The M1 had been closed at Meadowhall and the powers that be, with the assistance of a small army of bossy little cones, had funnelled me off the motorway and into the vast array of empty car parks that surround the huge shopping complex.

Normally when this happens I just follow everyone else until twenty minutes later we all pour back onto the motorway a mile or so nearer home. But it was getting on for midnight and there wasn't another soul about, so I had to take the responsibility upon my own shoulders. I wandered into and reversed out of several loading bays before I hit upon a likely-looking main road and was able to put my foot down once more.

I turned round in Rotherham and headed back towards Meadowhall but I never found the motorway again and so I went through the middle of Sheffield and then threaded my way through a series of little villages that were kind enough to shepherd me all the way home to Huddersfield.

The front path at this time of night is like a creeping nature reserve. Herds of wild slugs have slithered up from the cracks and crevices between the paving stones and are busy doing nothing in particular.

I find slugs the most repulsive of creatures and the thought of stepping all over them as I work my way up the garden path simply turns my stomach over. So I stand by the gate and jump up and down, waving my arms in the air, until the security lights decide to take notice. The slugs must think that this is some sort of war dance that magically turns night into day, which in a way I suppose it is.

I keep an old tablespoon stuck in the rockery and with this fearsome weapon I am able to scoop up the slugs and hurl them high over the hedge and out into Park Drive. That way I don't have to watch as the slimy little devils explode onto the tarmac and there is never a trace of them to be seen in the morning.

My wrist action is improving all the time and I rapidly cut my way through about half of them, sparing only a couple of snails who had pulled over for a few moments and rested their carapaces on the hard shoulder. I don't do snails – snails have mortgages.

I took a breather. It had been a long day and some of the slugs seemed to weigh in at around a pound and a half. I bent down to retrieve my tablespoon and caught my breath as I noticed a pair of wicked green eyes staring at me from under the holly bush.

'Nokia?'

'*Yeow.*'

I heaved a sigh of relief. Nokia I can handle. My first thought had been that this could be the mother of all slugs who was about to seek revenge by going straight for my throat.

There was a rustling of leaves and what appeared at first sight to be a small black bullock stomped out from under the bush.

'*Yeow.*'

Nokia's conversation might appear somewhat limited in cold print. In fact it also appears somewhat limited in real life, but the varied inflections of his myriad *yeows* open wide a picture-window on his whole personality and it's quite possible for the two of us to enjoy a more than healthy exchange of views.

We never touch on politics or religion. Other than that anything goes, even though our discussions usually boil down to the thorny subjects of cat food and fresh bedding.

Let me tell you about Nokia. Just over a year ago we enjoyed the intermittent company of a black feral tomcat called Eric. He would use our cellar as a refuge every now and then, whenever life seemed to be getting on top of him and he needed to get away from the wife and the kids for a few hours, chill out and then warm up his bum on the central heating boiler.

At first I could never get anywhere near him. As soon as I pushed open the inner cellar door he would be off out through the cat flap and up the stone steps, a blur of jet black fur and multicoloured teeth.

Over the months we arrived at an uneasy truce. I could pay him a brief visit as long as I didn't look straight at him. He would stiffen up on his boiler until he was almost twice his size, hair on end, his claws unsheathed and at the ready. With my back turned I would watch him through an old bathroom mirror that had been relegated below stairs. Cats never seem to have got the hang of mirrors.

He was a fine animal, of that there was no doubt, about two or three years old and as hard as nails. But he had clogged-up eyes and a nose to match and if he went on living wild in the park there weren't all that many months left in him. Sure enough, one day he disappeared and I never saw him again. Then a few days later an item appeared in the *Huddersfield Examiner*. The RSPCA had captured a pair of feral cats in the park and had them spayed, along with their three black kittens. It was hoped that good homes would soon be found for all of them. Unfortunately, however, a fourth kitten had escaped and was still living rough in Greenhead Park.

First thing next morning I went out into

the courtyard to switch on the fountain and there on the old wooden bench sat a half-grown kitten, as black as coal, looking as though he had walked straight from the page of a children's story book.

I sat down beside him and he backed away nervously.

'Hello, young man. I was reading about you only last night.'

'*Yeow.*'

'I think I knew your dad – slightly.'

'*Yeow.*'

I have a way with cats. It comes from years of experience and the secret lies in the tone of voice. It tells them they can trust me.

'*Yeow.*'

He had come a little closer now and I reached out to stroke him and reassure him that all his troubles were over.

The pain was excruciating. Nevertheless, after I had washed away all the blood, applied a generous coating of Savlon and carefully bandaged my hand, I went back out to show the kitten that we Longdens are a fearless tribe.

He'd gone, but I put a bowl of cat food down by the bench for him and within the hour that had disappeared as well. After that first meeting he came back on a twice daily basis. Sometimes he arrived in the morning looking as though he'd been drawn through a hedge backwards. On good days he looked as though he'd almost been drawn through a hedge backwards.

I reckoned he needed somewhere safe to sleep. I had recently cleaned up the cellar, decorated it and turned it into a gymnasium for Aileen, and now Eric had gone I had boarded up the cat flap, so I went to work on the small stone outhouse that nestles under the courtyard steps.

First I shifted out at least a couple of tons of white stone that was going to furnish the new rockery when I got round to it, then several barrowloads of soil and white chippings that had accumulated over the years. The outhouse has an earth floor and I solved that problem with a marble worktop that had been hanging around for years, looking for a mission in life. All this was done on bended knee and with buggered back – the space is only three foot high and I now have a strong fellow feeling with those Cornish tin miners of days gone by.

I found a wooden tea chest that would serve as a bedroom and furnished it with a wicker cat basket which I lined with a tiny sheepskin rug. The door would pose a problem for the kitten. He would never be able to reach the lock and whereabouts on his person would he keep the key? I solved the dilemma by replacing the battered old door with a lean-to that left him with a cat-sized space at the bottom.

I wondered how I was going to steer the vicious little ball of fluff towards his new quarters, but I needn't have worried. Over the past couple of days he had been keeping an eye on me as I worked on the renovation and that night, just before I went upstairs for a well-earned bath, I watched through the kitchen window as he sniffed around the makeshift door. My heart leapt as he disappeared inside.

An hour later, smelling sweetly of whatever it is that Aileen buys from the shopping channel, I went out to investigate. I eased back the lean-to very quietly and there all curled up in the basket was the little black kitten, out to the wide and snoring his tiny head off.

Since then I have added a kitchen in the shape of a sturdy weatherproof box that stands under cover by the back door, and in between his smart little bedroom and his bowl of nourishing Iams fish biscuits lies the little pond that is open all hours and provides an ever ready source of clear fresh drinking water.

If ever Iams require a male model to advertize their excellent wares they need look no further than the muscular moggie who was standing before me at a quarter to two in the morning.

'*Yeow.*'

His muscles rippled under the black fur that shone like oil in the moonlight. If I tried to stroke him these days he would have my arm off.

'I'm off to bed now, Nokia – I'm shattered.'

Aileen christened him Nokia. She's a mobile phone freak and she's convinced that he is Eric's son.

'*Yeow.*'

'Sorry. I didn't realize – I'll fill your dish up before I go to bed.'

'*Yeow.*'

'Don't mention it. See you in the morning.'

CHAPTER FOUR

I don't remember a thing about East-bourne. I know I set out to go there and I know I must have been there. I know that I gave a talk there because I had a cheque in my pocket and I knew I was on my way back from somewhere, so the chances are it was Eastbourne.

I also remember thinking as I headed back through the night to deepest Yorkshire that the most depressing sign on the M1 must be the one that will insist on telling me that I am on my way to 'Luton and the North'.

My God, if Luton is to the north there is still a hell of a long way to go before the countryside begins to roughen up and I am eventually eased from the motorway into the Meadowhall shopping complex once again.

I began to wonder how long it takes for jetlag to wear off. It was over a week since I arrived back from New York and I was still floating around in a sort of feathery never-never land, waiting for my head to clear customs.

Then the thought occurred to me that I could have been born with a rare type of jetlag that comes from floating around in a confined space for nine months – especially when you consider that the confined space in question was completely surrounded by my somewhat eccentric mother.

I needed a break. The white lines on the motorway were beginning to fray at the edges and go off on their separate ways as though they were expecting a tram to come along at any moment. I experimented with a short burst of rapid blinking and then found that if I kept just the one eye completely closed the white lines would quickly sort out their differences and get back together again.

Driving with one eye shut isn't really an option and yet there was nothing I could do about it until I arrived at the next exit, which must be all of thirteen miles away. The powers that be wouldn't have approved if I had stopped for a nap on the hard shoulder and so I carried on, first one eye and then the other, the car in front moving three feet to the left and then three feet to the right as I swopped over eyes.

This was dangerous. I remembered the old joke: 'He died peacefully in his sleep, but his passengers died shouting and screaming.' It wasn't funny. I didn't want to die yet and I certainly didn't want to take some poor innocent motorist with me.

I wound down both windows fully to let in more fresh air, and as I did so a sleek black hearse, as silent as the night, overtook me on the inside lane doing well over ninety miles an hour.

I was using my right eye at the time and so my nose was in the way, and I didn't catch sight of the apparition until it had raced effortlessly ahead of me. There was just a whoosh of air as it sailed off into the distance.

Well, it's not all that often that a hearse appears out of nowhere on the slow lane of the M1, streaks past you, and then belts off like the clappers at just after half past two in the morning, and believe me it's the sort of thing that clears the head wonderfully. A short sharp burst of adrenalin flooded my body and immediately my eyes were back on speaking terms with one another.

'Hey up, I can see properly.'

'Me an' all.'

I put my foot down so that I could catch up and grab a closer look. The hearse was obviously enjoying kicking its heels in this wild burst of freedom. No need to be sober and responsible at this time of night. It reminded me of the dutiful guide dogs who go all daft, roll on their backs and paw the air of Greenhead Park as soon as they are let off the leash for a few brief moments.

There was a coffin in the back of the

hearse but no wreaths and no flowers. The driver was in his shirtsleeves, his black jacket slung over the seat behind him.

Terry Pratchett would have us believe that Death roams the myriad worlds as a skeleton astride a white charger called Binky, carrying a scythe so thin you can see straight through it. Someone should tell Terry that things have moved on a bit since then. Death now roams the M1 with an ever-ready coffin in the back of a black Rolls-Royce. He is still a generous eighteen stone away from being a skeleton and he has a fag hanging out of the corner of his mouth.

Apparently my time hadn't yet arrived and so I waved goodbye to the hearse and turned off into the motorway service area to chance my arm once again, this time risking death either by food poisoning or from sheer boredom.

These places are all alike. It's not easy to tell one from another during the daytime, but in the middle of the night they take on an eerie sameness that defies description. I know – I've just spent well over an hour trying to describe it and failed miserably.

The walking dead were taking the weight off their feet, all of them sitting at their usual tables in the cafeteria, spaced well apart so that they wouldn't have to catch each other's eye or worse still speak actual words to another human being.

The tattooed man with the *Daily Mirror* and a mug of tea was there. He doesn't usually eat anything but tonight he had a little pile of Jaffa Cakes stacked up by his left elbow.

Two young women had taken the table by the artificial rubber plant. They were sitting across from one another, expressionless and as still as the night, each a mirror image of the other, staring down blankly at a mobile phone, only a tap-dancing thumb showing any sign of life as it expertly texted God-knows-what to God-knows-who at this time in the morning.

I bought a cup of coffee and a Kit Kat and went in search of a table where I wouldn't interfere with the spaced out pattern of the night visitors. On the way I passed close by a small ragged Irishman whom I have seen portrayed in many a film, most memorably by John Mills as the village idiot in *Ryan's Daughter*.

I smiled and added a friendly nod for good measure. He rewarded me a thousandfold with a huge grin that screwed itself into a gargantuan knot until it eventually ran out of steam and disappeared somewhere round the back of his neck.

I would have bet anything that there would be but a single tooth sticking out of those ancient Hibernian gums, maybe just a little off centre and to the left. But I would have been wrong. I was treated to an all singing, all dancing set of dentures that had a life of their own. They were having a ball in there, first breaking into a gentle Irish jig before roaring into a whirling finale that would have had Michael Flatley signing them up like a shot. The top set just had time for a farewell curtsey before the curtain came down and the show was over. I walked over to a table by a window, plonked down my cup and saucer and then went off looking for an ashtray.

I found one perched on a window sill by the mobile phone girls. They were still taking no notice of one another, texting frantically, their thumbs as busy as the Irishman's teeth. I held out the ashtray.

'All right if I take this?'

They stared up at me vacantly, as though I were bright green and had been beamed down from another planet.

I took that as a yes and trekked off back towards my table, and as I did so a somewhat sobering thought occurred to me. Perhaps I had done the two girls a great disservice. Maybe they were both hard of hearing and the text messages were a fresh and simple means of harnessing the new technology so that they could at least hold a semblance of a conversation with one another.

I made a mental note not to go jumping to

conclusions in the future and then immediately jumped to another as I spotted the
little Irishman making his way towards my
table.

*He's seen my ashtray and he's going to bum a
fag off me.*

He beamed once more. His dentures
shook with excitement and greeted me like
an old friend.

'Excuse me, sor. Could you spare me a
moment?'

'Of course.'

'Could you tell me. Is this the side of the
motorway that goes up, or is it the side that
goes down?'

'It's the northbound carriageway. The side
that goes up.'

'Ah, that's all right then. Only I keep
nipping back and forth over that little bridge
and then I end up forgetting which side I've
finished up on.'

'Where are you heading for?'

He pulled back the chair opposite and sat
down. His teeth hesitated for a split second
and then graciously decided to join him.

'They tell me I'm going to be working in
the North-East.'

'Whereabouts?'

'They haven't told me yet.'

'Well, you're going in the right direction.
As long as your car's over this side.'

'Oh, I don't have a car.'

He's going to bum a lift as well.

'They're picking me up in the car park here early on Friday morning.'

'It's only just turned into Thursday. You've got all night and tomorrow night as well to wait.'

'Ah, it's no problem. I like to be early and it's very comfortable here. I'm getting to know everybody and there's always a cup of tea to be had and you'd be surprised how much food people leave lying on the table.'

At that moment the two deaf girls pushed back their chairs and began to make their way out towards the shopping mall. My new-found friend cast his eyes professionally over the debris they had left behind them and began to rise expectantly. It looked quite promising.

Then he sat himself down again as one of the girls stopped in her tracks and turned back towards the table.

'Bloody hell. I've left me bleedin' coat.'

Her friend sighed dramatically. 'I don't know. You're not effin' fit to be let effin' loose.'

At least their silence had been golden. My companion started up again as the girls finally sailed off into the distance, only to be beaten to the table by a tall bald man in an apron who began to clear away the mess onto a tray.

You win some and you lose some, and the

54

Irishman took his defeat nobly with a simple shrug of the shoulders.

'The trouble is, you see. I've enough money for a cup of tea every now and then if I make it spin out, but I'm dying for a fag. I don't suppose you could see your way to offering me one.'

So I was wrong. He wouldn't dream of bumming a fag off me. I was going to offer him one. I took a pack of Dunhill International from my pocket, lit one for myself and passed the packet over. There were seven in there. He took one and I lit it for him. He took a deep drag and then made to push the cigarettes back across the table to me. I shook my head. I had a full pack in the car.

'You keep them.'

He tucked them deep inside a bulging poacher's pocket that seemed to have been added to his jacket as an afterthought.

'God bless you, sor. You're a real gentleman.'

Over the Irishman's shoulder I could see the tall bald man in the apron approaching, his tray now piled high with a wobbling mound of discarded this and leftover that.

He stopped by my companion's right elbow, and with a gentle grace that would have been an object lesson to many a West End waiter, he placed in front of the little Irishman a triangular plastic box that had in

55

its prime once held a pair of matching sandwiches, but now served as a see-through
home to the sole, but still sprightly, survivor.

'God bless you, sor. You're a real gentleman.'

The tall bald man in the apron cast an
expert eye over his heaving tray and then
butted up a six-pack of custard creams to
the side of the lonely sandwich. The fact
that the six-pack now held only two and a
half broken biscuits did nothing to diminish
the little man's obvious delight.

'A real gentleman.' He peeled open the
sandwich and peered inside. 'Bacon, lettuce
and tomato – now there's a fine combination.'

His benefactor smiled and without a word
left to carry on his reclamation work elsewhere. It seemed that we real gentlemen
were rather thick on the ground this Thursday morning.

It took quite a time for the Irishman to
polish off the sandwich. I don't think his
teeth were really up to it and he decided to
give them a rest before asking them to tackle
the custard creams. He jammed the biscuits
into his voluminous pocket and stood up.

'Can I get you a cup of tea, sor?'

I gave my coffee a stir to wake it up. 'No,
I'm fine, thank you.'

I watched him as he toddled off towards

the till desk. He ordered his drink and then, as the disinterested girl behind the counter turned her back to top up the teapot with hot water, I saw his hand dip expertly into a carton of biscuits or whatever that were sitting innocently by his right hand, just asking for it.

He took ages to pay for the drink, sorting through a little pile of copper coins as though they were his life savings – which, come to think of it, they probably were.

He toddled back to his original table, stopping every now and then to have a quick swig of the tea while it was still hot. His pocket, now pregnant with his ill-gotten gains, had taken on a life of its own and looked for all the world as though it were walking alongside him.

He gathered together his worldly possessions. A tattered newspaper, a little machine for rolling his own cigarettes and a table tennis bat. I was still trying to work out the significance of the table tennis bat when he appeared at my elbow. His pocket arrived just a few moments later, breathing heavily.

'I'm just off to have a look at the other side, sor.'

He bent and delicately placed a small pile of Jaffa Cakes by my coffee cup, then whispered in my ear.

'There you are, sor. A little something for you.'

And he was gone, out of my life for ever. ✗

It was time I was off if I was going to grab a couple of hours' sleep before Aileen stumbled into the new day. She's particularly vulnerable first thing in the morning and inanimate objects take advantage of her.

I walked over to the counter and dropped the Jaffa Cakes back in the carton whence they came, and as I did so the tall bald man in the apron pushed his way out through the kitchen door. The apron had gone, however, and now he wore an extremely well-cut suit together with a deep blue tie. He could have been mistaken for a solicitor or a bank manager if he hadn't had a large enamel bucket swinging from his left hand.

'Finished for the night?'

'Almost. Just one more little job to do.'

He slammed his hip against the bars of a door that sternly declared there was absolutely no exit. Apparently that only applied to the likes of me and he was through it and out into the night air almost without breaking step.

I made my way back to the table. I have left my mobile phone stranded on café tables throughout the length and breadth of Great Britain. A good percentage of my annual mileage must be taken up by retracing my steps in order to retrieve my mobile phone.

It was waiting patiently for me, lying on its

back by the little sachets of mustard and tomato sauce, and I could tell it was pleased to see me. I tucked it safely into an inside pocket and as I did so the security lights burst into life outside the window.

The tall bald man in the well-cut suit was striding along a narrow grass path that worked its way through a forest of bushes towards a line of assorted lorries that had done what they had to do and parked up for the night.

Behind him a ragged cat emerged from beneath a healthy-looking forsythia and then another from down the side of a shed. Other bushes produced other cats, some hanging back nervously, some almost bursting with energy, intent on being first in the queue.

I had never seen a herd of cats before. After a few moments there must have been thirty or so trailing in the wake of this pied piper and there were yet more who had anticipated this golden moment and were waiting for him up ahead. They rose out of the long grass and the more adventurous went forward to meet him, eyes firmly fixed on the enamel bucket.

He stopped and knelt down in a freshly mowed clearing, feeding some of the first arrivals by hand, then casting huge handfuls towards the shy and retiring who didn't like to intrude.

Not a single cat was left out. He had eyes

59

in the back of his head. From my wider perspective I could see the odd stray still lurking on the outer fringe, but before I could will him to turn round and take notice, each and every one of them had some part of a dead animal winging its way through the air towards them.

I must have stood there and taken in the scene unfolding before me for at least ten minutes. The cats were a motley assortment of stray and feral – black, white, ginger and tortoiseshell. Between them they would have lived through the equivalent of a Greek tragedy, but for the moment life was good and it was all down to a very decent man and his enamel bucket.

On the way out I passed by the tattooed man with the *Daily Mirror*. He had reached the back page. It had taken him well over an hour – which must be some sort of endurance record for the *Daily Mirror* – and he still had the little pile of Jaffa Cakes stacked up by his left elbow. I indicated the biscuits with a slight nod of the head.

'How many cigarettes did you give him?'
'Just the one.'

He'd worked out a far better deal than I had. That's my trouble – I'm just not hard enough.

CHAPTER FIVE

I sat at the kitchen table with my first coffee of the day and watched the blue tits as they set about furnishing their new home. They had been back several times to have a look at the hole in the stone wall but they didn't appear to be doing anything about it, and I had worried that some unscrupulous estate agent might have made them a better offer.

My neighbour Dave had put me right. He is on first name terms with most of the birds around here and his garden is a kind of Flamingo Land with frogs.

'You've screwed it up. You've made the opening too large. They like a tiny entrance with a bit of a drop behind it so that they are safe out of reach. Buy them a bird box.'

So I did. I hung one just above the hanging basket so that they would still have a front garden and in no time at all they were busy settling themselves in, adding the odd personal touch here and there until they had it just as they wanted.

Maurice would disappear for long intervals, returning eventually with some strange-shaped object he'd obviously picked up in Ikea. There was no doubt that Maureen was in overall charge of the operation and at times tempers became frayed and then Maurice would take off and sit sulking in the lilac tree.

Aileen appeared at my side, having showered and dressed.

'What colours am I wearing?'

'Sort of gold trousers and a bright purple top.'

'Good God.'

She disappeared to put matters right. Her wardrobe is colour coded and the system works perfectly most of the time, but just occasionally she will emerge from the bedroom looking as though she has recently set fire to herself.

I love being at home after a speaking tour. No more motorways for a while, no more having to dress up, just jeans and a T-shirt and lots of coffee with the morning papers.

The only fly in the ointment was that I had signed a contract to write a new book and it was time to get cracking. I had written just under three thousand words and rung Transworld to tell them that it was in the post.

'I've finished the first chapter.'

'Great. What's it about?'

'I go down to Sainsbury's.'

'What happens after that?'

'I come home.'

There was a distinct pause at the other end of the line.

'Right. I'll leave you to it then?'

The problem was that I had fallen out of the habit of writing. For a couple of years I hadn't been at all well. I was totally exhausted and ready for bed long before lunchtime. Sometimes my head didn't even bother to get up with me in a morning, just left me to it, and I would float around the kitchen trying to remember how you made toast.

I managed to complete the odd magazine article, which compared to putting together an eighty-thousand-word book is rather like competing in a ten-metre sprint as opposed to running the marathon.

Eventually the lovely Dr Helen sorted me out and nowadays, with the help of a daily cocktail of pills and a regular injection, I am more or less back in the swim of life, albeit splashing about in the shallow end.

I remember having had huge doubts as I set about working on my first book. All those years on the radio and I never thought twice about my skimpy education and the fact that I had failed every exam that ever came my way, from eleven-plus to O levels and practically everything else in between. I once attained a 100 per cent mark in gardening, but then I had caught the gardening master wrapping himself round the English mistress in the school greenhouse the week before.

Eventually the Manor School gave up on me and kindly turned a blind eye when I took an unofficial leave of absence so that I could work out what I wanted to do with the rest of my life. I never went back.

It wasn't until the air force and the wonderful Flight Lieutenant Cassell who came bursting into my life with his vast and eclectic collection of books that I embarked on a lifetime of voracious reading and began to cobble together a mishmash of a so-called education that still leaves a lot to be desired.

For instance, I am very conscious that I have never taken a deep breath and plunged myself into the complete works of William Shakespeare. I have often told myself that one day I will, but then the latest Bill Bryson arrives in the shops and I'm off and running in a completely different direction.

As I sat down to begin work on *Diana's Story* all those years ago, with only a battered old typewriter and the warm glow of ignorance in my corner, I came across a little verse that made me feel a lot better. I have no idea where it comes from and so I can't give the author the credit he or she deserves.

For years a secret shame destroyed my
    peace –
I'd not read Eliot, Auden or MacNeice.
But now I think a thought that brings me
    hope,
Neither had Chaucer, Shakespeare, Milton,
    Pope.

Aileen presented herself for inspection once
more, this time dressed from head to toe in
black – trousers and a silk shirt. She can't go
wrong in black. The contrast with her strawberry blonde hair is dramatic and it always
turns me on.

'Well?'

'You look terrific, love. There's just one
little thing.'

She had decided that just a touch of eye
shadow wouldn't go amiss, but instead of
applying it with the appropriate brush she
seemed to have plastered it on with a small
trowel.

For as long as it took me to get to work on
her with a damp flannel and a cotton wool
ball I was briefly married to a rather petite
and altogether much sexier version of the
Lone Ranger.

Whenever I need to conjure up a little inspir-
ation I go off on a walkabout. Nothing too
strenuous, and I always make sure that I have
some reason for leaving the house, otherwise

it might be misconstrued as exercise and that would never do. Fortunately there's always a letter that needs posting or a prescription that needs picking up from the chemist's.

The countryside round here is dramatic and wildly beautiful, but I usually go no further than just up the road to Marsh. I need human beings about me if I am to be drip-fed with a regular injection of that wonderfully precise way people have of expressing themselves around these parts.

Peach's chemist's shop is always a rich source. If there is a queue then so much the better. I can hang around and examine the labels on the antiperspirants whilst I hang my ears out to dry

But I had only gone as far as the Shell petrol station when a woman stopped me by plonking herself directly in my path.

'You've got a lot to answer for, you have.'

'I'm very sorry, love. What have I done?'

'Thanks to your books I've gone and saddled myself with a bloody cat. I wasn't his first choice. He went all the way down the other side of the street, sitting on people's doorsteps for hours on end, and nobody took pity on him. Then he started up our side. Just sitting there – waiting to be set on.'

I loved that 'waiting to be set on'. It brings with it images of yesteryear and mill workers walking the length of Occupation Road all the way up to Lindley in the early hours to hang around outside the factory gates, hoping to catch the foreman's eye. I could just imagine the little cat gluing himself outside the front door of house after house.

'*Give us a job.*'

He was probably hard at work at his new home as we spoke, about to start on the ironing, having already painted the back bedroom and done the washing up. The woman was beginning to move away. 'He's an ugly little bugger an' all, but he's good company. You have to admire triers, don't you?'

I carried on up the hill and just as I was approaching Exhibit, an elegant furniture shop that in days gone by was once the home of Mrs Singh's second-hand emporium, a young girl strode past me on the outside as though she was lapping me in the ten thousand metres, but then she had an unfair advantage.

She wore incredibly high heels. So high that she wasn't actually walking uphill, she was on the level. I wondered how she would cope with the return trip downhill and how she would manage to pull up at the traffic island.

Her legs were so long and her white microminiskirt so incredibly short that it drew gasps from two women who were window gazing. They turned and stared after her.

'I've seen longer vests.'

So had I but they weren't anywhere near as interesting. I put on a spurt to get a closer look, but she turned right into Croft House Lane and teetered out of my life for ever.

You win some and you lose some and I won the next round in the post office. There was a long queue that spilled out of the door and, after popping my letters in the postbox on the pavement outside, I fastened myself on the tail end. Soon I was trying to work out a snippet of conversation that came floating my way from a couple of women up near the front.

'I always put a sponge down the back myself – but then you've got goldfish, haven't you?'

The woman in front of me turned and gave me a quizzical smile, clearly also trying to squeeze some sense out of it. It was Sheila who works in Hair By Trudy and she's one of a closely knit team of four fearsome women who frighten the life out of me every Friday morning when I drop Aileen off to have her hair done.

Away from her natural habitat she seemed almost human and we chatted away happily until we had worked our way up to the front of the queue, at which point she began to worry that her wait might have been in vain. She approached the counter in some trepidation.

'I've just realized. I haven't any form of identification on me.'

'Why? What is it you're after?'

'I want to pick up my father-in-law's pension.'

The woman behind the counter hardly missed a beat. 'Do you know him?'

'Yes.'

'Oh well, that'll do then.'

I stopped off on the way back to have a chat with my good friend Alison who owns an Aladdin's cave of a shop called Don't Forget. She was dealing with a woman who had forgotten something very important.

'I must be the worst mother in the world.'

She went on to explain that her little daughter had lost a tooth the day before and put it under her pillow, fully expecting the tooth fairy to pay her a visit during the night.

But the worst mother in the world had been very busy and it had slipped her mind and there had been tears in the morning. Later that day the little girl had received an official fax sent directly from the tooth fairy's head office, saying that she was very sorry.

'I broke my wing yesterday morning and the doctor said that I mustn't fly for twenty-four hours until it gets better.' Apparently tooth fairies heal very quickly. The fax went on. 'I will be sure to pay you a call tonight and besides leaving you something for the tooth I will also pop a special little present under your pillow to make up for your disappointment.'

So the worst mother in the world was now on the lookout for the perfect little gift, the sort of thing that a recuperating tooth fairy with her wing in a sling might be able to manage.

We all thought long and hard and eventually settled on a tiny soft doll with a key ring sprouting from her head. Alison thought it would be perfect.

'The tooth fairy will be able to hang it round her neck whilst she's flying.'

Back in the real world I attached myself to the end of yet another queue, this time joining the walking wounded in Peach's chemist's shop.

I always find that the staff in there make me feel better the moment I walk in through the door, but today they had their work cut out. The symptoms being bandied about were alternately cringe-making and rather mysterious.

'It feels like somebody's just pushed a red hot poker up my bum.'

'When I went to bed last night I had terrible earache and this morning when I woke up my leg had gone all numb.'

Chris Holt, the owner, handed out both his advice and his potions in his usual cheerful manner and his supplicants went on their way with a spring in their step, feeling that with a bit of luck they might just live to see the end of the week.

By this time we had been joined by a rather odd couple. A tall, angular woman seethed and simmered under a wide-brimmed hat that I remember having seen once before, on Pathé News around the time of the Queen's coronation. Alongside her stooped an amiable-looking man, old before his time and a good foot and a half shorter than his wife. He wore what seemed to be a permanent apology of a half smile as his wife continually showed her disapproval at being kept waiting.

As the queue continued to creep slowly along she became more and more agitated, taking in deep breaths and then letting them out noisily and at length so that the rest of us would be left in no doubt that she was not amused by this unforeseen delay.

Eventually she snapped and glared down at her browbeaten husband.

'Right. I can't waste my time standing about here for ever. I'm going up to Hadfield's for the bread and after that I'll be in the Co-op. I'll meet you outside there and I don't want to see you coming out of that betting shop across the road. Do you hear?'

As she stormed out of the door an embarrassed silence fell over the queue. Looks were exchanged and eyebrows were raised.

The old man said nothing at first, but then with perfect timing he cleared his throat and declared, 'I don't know. I'll have to have her put down. She's too old to breed from and she's too vicious to keep as a pet.'

The bubble of tension that had taken over the small shop burst in a gale of laughter and business was resumed as normal.

Nokia was waiting for me as I pushed open the courtyard gate.

'*Yeow.*'

'Give me a minute, old son, and I'll be with you.'

'*Yeow.*'

'In a minute.'

I think I may have screwed up Nokia's life. He doesn't really know what he's all about any more. He is still a wild cat in theory and by rights he should be roaming free in the park, terrorizing all the soft domestic moggies in the vicinity and having his way with the more attractive females.

In fact all he does is pad softly between his bedroom under the steps and his cat kennel by the back door, pausing only to knock back a swift half every now and then from the ornamental pond before enjoying the luxury of a casual crap on the rockery. Food is no longer a moving target that wears a fur coat and travels on all fours at great speed. It appears mysteriously twice a day, in a chipped white bowl not six inches away from the door of his kennel.

We have long chats about this and that – the political situation in the Middle East, the effect Wayne Rooney might have on the England team once he's back to full fitness – and Nokia purrs and pounds the paving stones with pure pleasure, and yet I still can't get within a foot of him without him having a go at me with his vicious claws.

'Right. Now what is it?'

'*Yeow.*'

He turned and trotted across the court-yard towards the pond. I followed at a discreet distance until he stopped abruptly, sat down and stared in the general direction of his bedroom.

There was his blanket, lying stranded on the paving stones in no man's land, a couple of yards from his sleeping quarters. Every now and then, first thing in the morning or after he's had his afternoon nap, his claws get entangled in his blanket and it takes him some time to shake it off. I once found it hanging from the hedge by the rockery.

I took a detour round him and knelt down, tucked the blanket back in his basket and fluffed it up for maximum comfort.

'There we are, sorted.'

He came slowly towards me to have a closer look, to see if I'd made a proper job of it, and I couldn't help thinking that maybe this was a breakthrough. After all, he'd made a special point of telling me about it. Perhaps at last I had pulled the thorn from the lion's paw.

He settled himself down beside me, pounding the ground with his front paws to show his appreciation, and then, with a show of agility that I hadn't seen in him since he was a kitten, he lashed out at me and raked his claws down the length of my right thigh.

I chased him out of the courtyard and down the path until he scuttled under the camellia bush and buried himself beneath the lower branches that back up to the stone wall.

'*Yeow*.'

He knows I can't get at him when he's tucked under there and so do I, not without a stout pair of gloves and a pitchfork, and since I didn't have a pitchfork concealed about my person I had to content myself with reading him the riot act, which I did at great length.

'*Yeow*.'

That came across with a semblance of a sneer attached, very much a 'Yeow and whose army?'

I raised my tone a few notches until I

noticed that a considerable amount of blood was seeping through my jeans.

'I'll deal with you later.'

Once in the kitchen I slipped off my jeans to see what the damage was, and as I did so Tigger ambled across from her bed by the radiator to have a look at my bare feet.

She's always shown a great interest in my feet. I think she wonders how on earth I manage to balance on just the two alone and can't quite work out what has happened to the other pair.

It was good to see her up and about. She had hardly eaten a thing these past few days and was obviously feeling decidedly under the weather. If she wasn't any better in the morning I would take her to the vet.

In the meantime I concentrated on my own wounds. Nokia's claws had gouged four deep furrows in my thigh, one of which was bleeding profusely. I Dettoled and Savloned and bandaged as best I could and wondered what the hell I was going to do with Nokia. I couldn't allow him to go on like this.

Tigger grunted, a strange gargling noise that I had never heard from her before. I picked her up and plonked her on the draining board. Watching the taps run at close quarters is a particular hobby of hers.

Now she was up off the floor I could see

that all was not well. Her face seemed strangely distorted. I moved in close, eyeball to eyeball, for a better look, and it was as though she had swallowed a small rugby ball, sideways.

Her left cheek was terribly swollen, her left eye almost closed and her mouth clamped tightly shut. Her lips merely trembled as she tried to tell me about it. All that came of them was yet another gargling grunt.

Never mind about taking her to the vet tomorrow. We needed the vet to come and have a look at her here, as soon as possible.

CHAPTER SIX

Helen and Elizabeth arrived within the hour. We had never dealt with their practice before. Mrs Roger, who had always taken care of the cats, had recently retired along with her battered old leather bag and I had resorted to the Yellow Pages.

Whenever Tigger has been forced to have dealings with the medical profession she has always preferred to be examined by a woman than a man, but today she was in no mood to be pleasant to anyone and she hissed and snarled as they attempted to look her over. Helen tried to calm her down, to no avail.

'She's obviously in a lot of pain.'

They discovered the odd lump hanging from her undercarriage, but no way was she going to let them look in her mouth.

'We'll have to take her back to the surgery. We're going to have to put her out before we can examine her.'

As they eased her gently into a well-used cat transporter, Helen tried to prepare me for the worst.

'She's quite old, you know – there is a chance that she may not survive the anaesthetic.'

But the alternative didn't bear thinking about.

Aileen and I saw them out of the front door, Helen, Elizabeth and Tigger, our loyal old friend of seventeen years. Maybe this would be the last time we would ever see her. It was no way to say goodbye.

I tried to stroke her paw through the wire bars, but she didn't want to know me. She turned her back and curled up at the far end.

'We'll look after her,' Elizabeth murmured.

Helen hoisted the contraption into the car and promised that she would ring the moment she had any news.

And they were gone.

I shut the front door and Aileen and I collapsed into each other's arms and cried unashamedly. Then we drank a tasteless cup of coffee and tried to lift each other's spirits.

'She'll be fine.'

'Of course she will.'

Thermal had been hard at work down in the cellar, breaking in a brand new wicker ironing basket. Whenever we buy anything new he feels it is his duty to test it thoroughly by going to sleep in it for an hour or two, or three. He must have thought he had done a good job because he came up to tell us all about it and then, exhausted by the magnitude of a task successfully completed, he staggered over to his oil-fired radiator and settled down on his sheepskin rug for a well-earned rest.

I switched on my laptop, telling myself that time would pass that much more quickly if I got down to some work, but the words that came up on the screen wouldn't sort themselves out into any reasonable order and so I put the machine to bed and went out to do some weeding.

I find weeding to be one of the most therapeutic occupations I know. I can think beautiful thoughts whilst I'm weeding and the end results are usually most satisfying. When I come across that awkward little devil, the weed who punches his own weight and refuses to take it lying down, then I can take all my pent-up emotions out on him. The hooked knife comes out of my jeans pocket and a shiver runs through the whole length of the recalcitrant plant.

'Right, you little bastard.'

The bass beat of a car radio parked itself noisily across the road. The car arrived to join it a few moments later. The car engine was promptly switched off. The radio wasn't.

Ignore it. It'll be gone in a few minutes.

I went round to the back of the house and in through the courtyard gate in order to put the 100-year-old solid stone structure between me and the racket outside, but the *boom, boom, boom, boom* followed me round the corner, somewhat muted now but still as insistent.

I cracked and went out to have a word with them.

'Sorry, mate, didn't think.'

The radio snapped off and peace fell over Greenhead Park once more. It wasn't usually as simple as that.

I win some and I lose some, but rarely do I triumph so quickly. It wasn't until I turned back in through the gate that I realized I still had the hooked hunting knife in my hand. Must try that again.

Anyway, there would be more to do. The pair of them were eating fish and chips out of a copy of yesterday's *Daily Mirror* and drinking from a shared bottle of beer. They didn't look the sort who would go searching for a rubbish bin.

The car revved up, the radio snapped back into action and they were off, bouncing high over a sleeping policeman. As they did so a hand popped out of the passenger window and bundle of half-eaten fish and chips parachuted down onto the pavement.

As it landed the screwed-up frills of paper began to unfurl like some exotic flower in the height of summer until the congealed mass of fish, chips and *Daily Mirror* news-print opened itself up to the whole wide world. It wouldn't stay like that for long. The starlings would soon be in there, fighting amongst themselves for titbits, spreading their treasure all over the pavement.

I went out through the gate to tip the whole sorry mess into the rubbish bin and then stopped abruptly and sat down on the bottom step.

A squirrel had beaten me to it. He was sitting by the squishy packet, squatting on his haunches, back straight as a ramrod, holding a single chip between his front paws and nibbling away contentedly.

'Could do with a drop more vinegar.'

Even so, his tombstone front teeth shredded their way down the chip in no time at all and he eagerly bent to select another.

He didn't rush it. He first considered this one and then carefully contemplated that one. Eventually he decided on the one over there, the sort of chip that makes you proud to be British. A good four inches long, square as a country fence post and with just a touch of russet in all the right places. I rather fancied it myself.

I must have sat and watched him for a good ten minutes. Halfway through his lunch a couple of lovers strolled by and he nipped out of the way, sitting on the low wall that stops the park from fraying at the edges until they had gone past. The lovers only had eyes for each other, seeing neither the bag of chips nor the nervous little squirrel, and in no time at all he was back, tucking into his packed lunch with his usual impeccable pavement manners. I was reminded at that moment that by picking up litter I could almost be accused of interfering with the balance of nature, a lesson that had been brought home to me not long before.

For more years than I care to remember I have been out at night, picking up the half-eaten remains of a chicken tandoori masala here, a flurry of BBQ chicken wings there, and without fail at least two and a half inches of a seven-inch deep-pan pizza with extra pepperoni and a side order of garlic bread.

We suffer especially badly because we live right opposite a peaceful and most beautiful park and drivers like to pull in and eat their takeaway meals in these quiet and gentle surroundings, drinking in the delightful view laid out in front of them before they fire up the engine and hurl the remnants of their prawn vindaloo right across the road.

Sadly I have almost come to think of that as normal behaviour. What I could never understand was that often, in a morning, after I had cleaned up the varied heap of comestibles into the wire litter bin the night before, leaving just the solids for the already overworked street cleaner to tidy away, the bin would be half emptied, surrounded by a knee-deep sea of assorted rubbish. What sort of twisted mind would even think of doing that?

Then, in the early hours of one morning, I was out and about trying to persuade the cats that perhaps it was time they came in, put away their toys for the night and went off to bed. When I eventually found them, they were sitting on the garden wall, silently watching a painfully thin dog fox digging deep into the bin, scattering the contents all over the pavement.

I had screwed up his supper. He'd promised the wife and kids that he would bring home a pizza on his way back from the pub and that idiot across from the park had gone and buried the lot in this damned wire contraption. Didn't he ever think? ✗

The squirrel was still at it, contentedly nibbling away at yet another chip. What he didn't know was that a large black crow was now perched on the wall behind him, sizing up the situation and waiting to take over.

He moved in, shuffled up beside the squirrel and grabbed hold of a beakful of chips from the greasy paper. No table manners at all. The squirrel panicked, turned and shot off over the low wall and into the park, scrambling up the nearest tree, where he sat and fumed, angry as much with himself as with the crow.

'*What am I – a squirrel or a mouse?*'

It took him some time to decide which, but eventually he took a deep breath and trotted back headfirst down the tree trunk, then sat on the wall for a moment or so to compose himself.

'*I'm getting too old for this.*'

The crow was having to fiddle with a length of fish skin. He had it trapped under his foot and was tearing at it with his beak. The problem was that it was stretching like a piece of elastic and for the moment it engaged his total concentration.

So at first he didn't notice the squirrel sneak up beside him and grab another chip. When he did he obviously wasn't too pleased, but the squirrel stood his ground and eventually the two of them settled on an uneasy truce, an unlikely twosome tucking into an even more unlikely-looking lunch.

I left them to it. I wanted to ring the vet to find out how Tigger was getting along, but they had promised to let me know as soon as they had any news and I was sure they would keep their word.

The phone rang as I made a cup of coffee, but it was my daughter Sally reporting in on her return from a holiday in France.

'Hi, Dad. We've just walked in the house this minute. We had to make a detour to pick up Poppy from the kennels.'

Poppy is a rescue greyhound. A nervy, forty mile an hour couch potato who had been very badly treated before Sally and Steve adopted her and still can't believe that life can be this good, so is absolutely sure that it will all fall apart at the seams again any minute now. She hates being put in the boarding kennels and assumes that she must have done something awful and this is the beginning of the end.

'Steve's taken her out for a run on the Downs.'

There are a good half a dozen greyhounds who meet up there every day. Their owners let them off the lead and they run like the wind, lap after lap after lap, until they are absolutely knackered. One of the greyhounds has only three legs, but still manages to keep up with the leading pack – until she tries to turn on a sharp corner, at which point she cartwheels over and over again and lands up spreadeagled in the bushes.

'How did she cope with the kennels?'

'Much better this time, they say. But she didn't eat a lot – she's lost a dress size.'

I lit a cigarette and stared across at the phone, willing it to ring again. But it took not the slightest notice of me. It very rarely does if I am within spitting distance. It takes great pleasure in catching me out whenever

I am sitting on the lavatory with my trousers down round my ankles or am covered in mud up at the far end of the garden. It's a newcomer, it's digital and it's getting above itself.

As I reached out to flick my cigarette in the ashtray I noticed the bowl of bananas sitting by the coffee machine.

The bananas had experienced a make-over. In the morning post Aileen had received a set of black marker pens especially designed for those with little or no sight. They applied a thick black ink with a slightly raised surface that could be read with the fingertips and she had been practising.

Most of the bananas had a bold black *BANANA* written right down the whole of their length. Sometimes it would be a ***Banana*** and there was just one odd **Banana** cuddled up next to a solitary apple.

The apple had *APPLE* written in capitals all the way round its surface, obviously so that Aileen wouldn't make the mistake of thinking it was a *BANANA*. I was playing with the idea of nipping out and buying her a bunch of grapes – she loves a challenge – when the phone suddenly burst into life and my heart stood still.

'Mr Longden?'

'Yes.'

'Deric Longden, the writer?'

'Yes.'

'Oh, you won't remember me.'

She told me her name and I didn't remember her. But at least my heart slipped back into gear and I settled down for a journey into the unknown.

'You once brought your mother into Chesterfield Royal Hospital in the days before it moved, do you remember that? I was the one what syringed her ears.'

I did remember her. Sad, isn't it?

She was a student nurse, rather plain but with a wonderful bum. I can't remember names, but I never forget a bum. This one had hovered inches away from my face as she leaned over in the small cubicle to hand back the gift of hearing to my mother. It must have been all of twenty years ago.

'I just wanted to tell you that I met your cousin Geoff in Hathersage last Sunday and he asked to be remembered.'

'Really? How is he?'

'He's very well except he's just buried his wife and his knees are playing him up again.'

'I didn't even know his wife had died. That's terrible.' There are too many old friends and relatives who seem to slip out of your busy life as the years pass by. They are the entries on your Christmas card list that don't have a postcode. But why didn't he drop me a line? I would have made sure to be at the funeral.

'He said to tell you that he still goes up to

Saltergate on a Saturday to watch Chesterfield and you're not to feel guilty about not
keeping in touch.'

But I did feel guilty. Very guilty.

'Anyway, I must be going. I just thought
you'd want to know.'

And she rang off.

I sat at the kitchen table and worried about
Geoff and tried to remember what his wife's
name had been. I couldn't for the life of me
think what it was. That's unforgivable. I
couldn't even build up a picture of her in
my mind. Or of Geoff for that matter.

Then it slowly dawned on me that I don't
have a cousin Geoff. I have never had a
cousin Geoff. I have a cousin Denis and I
have a cousin Gordon and I have seen them
both in the last year and Audrey and Mavis
are still fighting fit and could leave me
standing in a five-metre sprint. There's a
cousin Michael living somewhere or other,
but I have never ever had a cousin Geoff.

I was still trying to make sense of it all when
the phone burst into life once more and
insisted that I deal with it immediately.

'Hello?'

'Mr Longden?'

'Yes.'

'This is Helen from the Calder Veterinary
Group.'

'How is she?'

'She'll be fine. Out like a light at the moment, but she's much tougher than she looks.'

I was glad I was sitting down. The relief that swept over me made me feel weak at the knees.

'She had a very nasty root abscess. We had to dig very deep and then remove most of her teeth. Her mouth was in quite a mess. Now she has only the two incisors at the back and just a few of the little teeth at the front. We have also removed that large lump round her nipple.'

'I don't know how I didn't notice sooner.'

'That's the trouble with cats. They're too brave for their own good.'

'When can I pick her up?'

'Give her a couple of hours and we'll check her over.'

'Thank you so much.'

'Oh, and we cut out a cyst from inside her lip and whilst she was out we treated an in-growing toe nail and trimmed all her claws...'

So that's why she had been strutting around like a ballet dancer these past few weeks.

'...and we've given her a short back and sides and shaved out the knots. She looks rather strange. I'll see you around seven.'

I went over to share the good news with Thermal. For the past few years the two had been inseparable. They slept together, they woke up together, one wouldn't even start a meal without the other being there, and yet today he hadn't even seemed to notice that she was missing.

Whatever, he was obviously pleased to hear that she had survived her ordeal. He purred and stretched happily as I told him that she would be back in a couple of hours or so. Or maybe that was just because I happened to be scratching his undercarriage at the time.

Cats are strange animals. Incredibly selfish and surprisingly caring in turn. It was then that I noticed that for the first time in his life he was stretched out on Tigger's personal sheepskin rug in front of Tigger's own tiny radiator. Was he showing that he was missing her, or was it merely a case of the grass being greener on the other side?

I was there just before seven. I only had to wait a few moments before I was ushered out of the waiting area and into a business-like side room, complete with well-scrubbed table, various implements of the trade and the impressively capable Helen, who placed a mobile cat transporter on the table.

The occupant was obviously far from mobile. 'Come on, Tigger.'

Tigger wasn't going anywhere. Helen tilted the box slightly and out slid a comatose cat who bore a strong resemblance to Tigger on a bad hair day.

'Hello, Tigger.'

At the sound of my voice she struggled drunkenly to her feet and immediately fell over. Helen helped her up, steadied her and then gently ran her hands over the little body, finishing off her inspection by holding Tigger's jaws apart and examining the inside of her mouth.

'It's not a pretty sight, but it looks quite healthy. Bring her back tomorrow and I'll see how she's going on and give her another injection.'

Tigger didn't like the sound of that. She tried to wriggle free and fell over once more, this time exposing her shaven little belly and the whole of her port side to the heavens. A row of neat stitches decorated her under-carriage and on her side, where once she had sported her crowning glory of the most beautiful and intricate tortoiseshell hair, was what looked like the marked-out instructions for a Readicut rug.

This time she struggled to her feet unaided and staggered towards her cat transporter. At the door she turned and glared hard at Helen before collapsing once more.

'Tortoiseshells,' said Helen, shaking her head. 'The redheads of the feline world.'

CHAPTER SEVEN

It had been a good day. My new satellite navigation system had talked me right out of the garage.

'Turn round.'

I did as I was told and then it talked me all the way through the ninety-one complicated miles to a lovely country hotel bang in the heart of Lincolnshire. As I pulled into the imposing driveway a finishing line appeared on the screen and the device signed off with a deservedly smug smile.

'You have arrived at your destination.'

My birthday present from Aileen was going to make life so much easier from now on. Just a few weeks ago I had driven all the way down to Yeovil to help launch the new Iams range of dry cat food, only to become completely lost in the last two hundred yards.

It happened time after time. Talks in Birmingham were becoming the stuff of nightmares. I remember once asking directions after I had been going round in circles for what seemed a lifetime. The man pointed above his head to a road that appeared to be hanging out of the sky.

'You want to be up there.'

'How the hell do I do that?'

'God knows. If I were you I'd leave that thing here and hop on a bus.'

The talk went well, the Lincolnshire ladies were delightful, I sold a lot of books and they paid me on the nail. Even the teatime crush on the M62 that forever wraps itself round the city of Leeds couldn't dampen my spirits.

My navigation system had led me by the hand all the way from Woodhall Spa.

'Three hundred yards. Cross the island. Take the third exit.'

If anything it was too perfect. All I had to do was sit there and steer. I wondered if perhaps I could humanize it a little.

'I tell a lie. It's the second exit. How silly of me – oh, I'm awfully sorry.'

'Don't worry. We all make mistakes.'

Or perhaps, *'Could we stop off at a Little Chef, please? I'm bursting.'*

Even though I knew how to get home perfectly well from here I let the little machine direct me every inch of the way. It seemed to take life so very seriously and I didn't want to hurt its feelings.

I wondered if it might take me off the M62 at the first Huddersfield exit, which is the long way round, but no – this baby knew exactly what it was about and ignored it completely. At junction 24 however it spoke loud and clear.

'In three hundred yards – take the next exit.'

'Right you are.'

'Take the exit.'

I took the exit and gave the machine a pat. 'Well done.'

I like to think that at that moment the two of us bonded and became a formidable team, a man and his machine who would be able to take these British Isles by the scruff of the neck and go where no man and his machine had gone before. Even perhaps, one day, right into the centre of Birmingham.

We were coming up to my favourite crossroads in the whole wide world. Fortunately the lights were at red and so I had the time to enjoy them for a few brief moments and to share them with my new friend.

For some strange reason Aileen and I make up characters from the signposts we see as we travel the length and breadth of the country. It helps allay the boredom and I had already come across a slight variation of this in Lincolnshire. A startling reflection in the glass windows of a bus stop: *Snotrag*. I glanced across the road and there was a village shop – Gartons.

But this little crossroads on the Halifax road leading down into Huddersfield was where it had all started. The signpost to the left directs the traveller towards Birkby and Fartown. The signpost to the right steers them up the hill towards Lindley and Salendine Nook.

Some twenty years ago, when we first laid eyes on these signposts, Aileen's mind immediately swung into Barbara Cartland mode and conjured up a picture of the imposing, but now slightly florid and overweight, Lieutenant Colonel Sir Birkby Fartown riding out at dawn to challenge my own champion, the Right Honourable Sir Lindley Salendine-Nook, to a duel. They probably fought it out right there on the stone pavers, in the shadow of the Cavalry Arms.

I have never had time to congratulate the victor. As usual a car horn from behind informed me that the lights had now changed and would I please extract my finger and get the hell out of here.

That's the trouble with car horns. They are so insistent, and they instantly condemn the victim. What we need is a catalogue of sounds from which we can select the appropriate message, just as we can with the ring tone on a mobile phone. They could range from '*You great stupid moron, are you trying to get us all killed?*' right down through the scale to a polite '*Excuse me, but there's a yard and a half of camel hair coat trapped in your driving door.*

Just thought I would mention it.'

Little sat-nav led me by the hand all the way home, right up to the front door.

'You've arrived at your destination.'

I thanked him, unplugged him and pre-pared to take him inside with me so that I could shove an electric charge up his bottom, ready for our next trip into the unknown.

The cats would be waiting for me just inside the hall doorway. They seem to know the sound of the car. They always see me off, sitting a certain distance away from the door so that it just brushes past their col-lective noses as I close it.

I once liked to imagine that they missed me so much that they would sit there, rooted to the same spot, faithfully awaiting my return. They are always there waiting for me, plonked in exactly the same place – a mere nostril's width away from a bad nose day. But Aileen tells me that isn't the case at all. As soon as they hear the outer door shut they immediately footle off back to their respective radiators.

'Good God. I thought he'd never go.'

'He's slowing down a bit, isn't he?'

'He's certainly not getting any younger.'

Apparently Thermal is the one who knows about cars. Visitors come and visitors go and the cats don't even move a muscle, with Thermal directing operations.

'*Relax. It's not him. That's a Ford Galaxy – 2.3 litre.*'

But the moment I pull up outside the house they are on their feet and out into the hall as fast as their arthritic limbs can carry them.

'*Don't forget it's your turn to purr this time.*'

'*I purred last time.*'

'*No you didn't. You rubbed up against his leg.*'

'*You're thinking of last Thursday.*'

As I pushed my way into the hall I saw that only Thermal had made it today. He swayed back expertly, bum stapled to the hall carpet, as the door swept past his nose. I gave him a great big scratch and he purred and then sniffed long and hard at where a small black kitten had velcroed itself to my right ankle in the Lincolnshire car park.

'*Mmm! Kitten, black with white trim. Female – five to six months old. Bit of a tart – had rabbit for breakfast.*'

'Come on, let's go and see how Tigger's coping.'

She lay flat out by her radiator, completely oblivious of the fact that she was being examined at close quarters both by her owner and the busy little nose of a feline of the opposite sex.

'She'll probably sleep a lot for the next few days,' the vet had told me.

And she had. Basically all the time. I had taken her down to the practice early that morning for a check-up. I hadn't needed the cat carrier. She'd slept in a blanket, all the way there and all the way back, waking only to growl and glare her way through the injection.

They had given me a few tins of special cat food which had been designed to be easily digested by a cat with a sore mouth, but Thermal had made life even easier for her by eating the whole of the first tin on her behalf and she had seemed grateful that he had taken over the responsibility. Thermal settled down on his sheepskin rug beside her.

'*I'll keep an eye on her.*'

'Thank you.'

'*My pleasure.*'

I made my way up to Aileen's study to see how her writing day had gone. She was busy rapping out instructions to her computer and I kept quiet so as not to confuse the two of them. After a while she sensed I was there.

'Go to sleep.'

The computer did as he was told and slammed his little door tight shut, glad to be able to snatch a few moments off and maybe grab forty winks, catch up on his ironing or whatever. Aileen looked up at me, anxious to be back in the heart of her story and not wanting me to take her mind off on some sort of trivial detour.

'Just thought I'd remind you that we're going out tonight.'

She didn't need reminding. She never forgets a thing. It can be really annoying at times.

'I know.' She turned back to her computer. 'Wake up.'

The computer immediately snapped into action. Poor little devil, he wouldn't have been able to get much ironing done. Hardly time for him to press his best pair of underpants. Come to think of it, he sounds exactly the sort of computer who would press his underpants.

I left her to it, reflecting on the fact that I very rarely take her anywhere. It's not for the sake of trying.

In the past few years we've been to Dubai, New York, France, Bratislava, all home to many wondrous sights which of course are all completely lost on Aileen.

'There's the Eiffel Tower.'

She would stare up at nothing in particular. As far as Aileen is concerned it might as well be an electricity pylon.

'Very nice. Can we go for a coffee now.'

I felt much better about this after we had made a return trip to the Writers' School at Swanwick where we first met some twenty years ago and I overheard two old friends talking about their recent trips abroad.

Colin said that he had taken his wife round

a leprosy museum somewhere or other and I was just thinking that he certainly knew how to spoil a girl when Bill butted in and said that he and his wife had been over to Bratislava to have a look at the museum of wardrobes. Maybe Aileen is right to avoid such excitement now that we are getting that bit older.

Over the years I have learned that the company of good friends, good food and a glass or two of wine round a familiar table are what she most appreciates and Tuesday nights are kept aside expressly for that purpose.

Five or so years ago the Tuesday Club more or less formed itself. There are eight of us, four couples, and for once there's none of that 'like her, can't stand him' nonsense about our get-togethers. We all get on like a house on fire.

We take it in turns to do the catering and so for the best part of a month all I have to do is to turn up with a bottle of wine. Then on the fourth week it's my turn to panic once more and come up with something to eat. They are all very good and never complain, but I have learned that cooking for eight is no mere matter of providing four times as much as one would for the two of us.

We all have our regular seats round the table and in that way Aileen doesn't become confused. She recognizes each voice and knows exactly where it's coming from.

Alison's husband Paul takes over my usual responsibilities for the night and sits next to Aileen, seeing to it that she gets her fair share of whatever is going.

'...and your Brussels are at nine o'clock. There's steak and kidney pudding right in the middle of your plate, broccoli is at seven o'clock and you've just dropped your fag ash in amongst your baked potatoes. Would you like gravy with that?'

Martin and Gillian sit opposite each other. To the uninitiated Martin might come across as a man of few words, but then anyone sitting next to Alison would find it difficult to get a word in sideways. Gillian is seated at the middle of the table, in that unfortunate position where it seems it would be much easier for all concerned if she were to dish out the food to the rest of us, so we let her get on with it and take not the slightest notice of her when she says that we take her for granted.

At the moment Mike and Jean are usually the last to arrive. They are moving their entire business to a vast warehouse on the other side of town and the steam rising from Mike's ears is an indication that perhaps all has not gone too smoothly today. Jean wearily plonks herself down next to Martin and from now on he is going to have his work cut out even thinking for himself,

101

never mind putting it into words. Stuck in there between Alison and Jean must be like sitting in a wind tunnel.

After all these years we have no need of one of those polite periods of adjustment whilst we weigh up the assembled company. We all know what the state of play was this time last week and simply take it from there.

Aileen sometimes finds it difficult to inject herself into the conversation. The rest of us can see the speaker's face as they are in full flow.

She'll be taking a breath any minute now.

And the moment they do – in we go. My problem is that I've reached the age where I often forget what I was about to say, and that can be fatal as the others have no shame and immediately take over my slot.

Aileen has recently developed a technique which involves leaning forward slightly and clearing her throat in a rather majestic manner. It wouldn't work for me, but the other Tuesday Club members have a soft spot for her and generously hand her the floor.

After a couple of glasses of white wine Mike's blood pressure will have settled itself down in the low two hundred and thirties which is pretty healthy for him and he will be matching Paul, insult for insult. By now the casual observer will have noticed that Martin isn't exactly a man of few words. It's simply that he only speaks when he has something to say, which wouldn't do for me.

Alison has developed a wonderful technique for injecting herself into the conversation, which alongside a strong personality, a ready wit and an extremely loud voice works wonderfully well.

'So...'

And on that signal we all shut up immediately and await yet another gripping instalment of the ongoing, everyday story of Huddersfield folk, with special reference to the area of Marsh and the Don't Forget gift and card emporium.

Tonight we were all giving ourselves a break and had arranged to meet in the Café Pacific, a very comfortable little restaurant tucked away under the railway arches, just outside the town centre.

'So...'

Alison launched herself into her story. Apparently, halfway through that afternoon a shifty young man had strolled into the shop, aimlessly picking up this and that and generally roaming around the place in a rather suspicious manner. Alison kept a weather eye on him whilst she dealt with another customer and he was obviously well aware he was being watched.

Eventually he disappeared up the stairs to try his luck on the next floor, unaware of the fact that she was monitoring his movements on the closed-circuit television. She didn't actually see him pick anything up but her suspicions were mounting by the minute and when he came downstairs again he seemed to have changed shape somewhat. She moved from behind the counter to find out why he somehow seemed to have put on a pound or two, and he suddenly made a dash for the door.

As he wrestled with the handle a two-foot-tall teddy bear fell out from under his coat and landed on the floor at his feet. He hesitated for a brief moment and then darted out of the shop and leapt on a passing double-decker bus. He threw his fare at the driver, raced upstairs and disappeared from view, no doubt congratulating himself on making his escape.

Unfortunately for him the driver had stopped in order to pick up some passengers who were waiting at the bus stop right outside Alison's shop door. The West Indian driver was just about to pull away when she scrambled on board.

'Don't you go anywhere. I'm after a shop-lifter.'

'OK.'

She marched upstairs and spotted him sitting in the middle of the long seat right at the back of the bus.

At this point in the story I began to feel a smidgen of sympathy for the shoplifter. To be trapped there with nowhere to go and to see this formidable ex-policewoman and bailiff, bosom heaving and eyes blazing, striding up the aisle towards him. If I had been in his position I would have wet myself.

He opened his coat and tamely handed her another large teddy bear.

'Anything else?'

'No.'

'Sure?'

'Yes.'

'Right. If ever I see your ugly face round here again then you won't be able to walk for a week. Do you get that?'

'Yes.'

Then, triumphantly flourishing the teddy bear aloft, she marched downstairs and smiled at the driver.

'You can go now.'

'OK.'

Alison thoroughly enjoyed her round of applause and then we all went back to the present task in hand, namely that of trying to catch the eye of the waiter.

The meal had been fine and we'd all enjoyed being out on the town, but the service that evening was incredibly slow. For some reason, unusually for a Tuesday night, the restaurant was absolutely packed and they were rather short on waiters. The owner had given most of his staff the night off and was coping on his own, with the help of a young trainee who was learning the business and still had some way to go.

The two of them were running here, there and everywhere, heads down, eyes firmly fixed on the plates they were carrying, desperately trying not to see the forest of raised arms that were trying to attract their attention.

We had some sympathy for the owner. We knew him well and his service was usually spot on, but we were becoming desperate for our coffee. We developed a special technique of synchronized arm-raising the second he appeared on the floor, Paul being the officer in charge.

'Now!'

Seven arms shot up in unison. In a perfect world it would have been eight, but Jean had her head down and was mucking about with her mobile phone. You are either a team player or you're not.

For a moment we thought we had him, but no. Head down, he was back on his way to the kitchen and we were just about to call it a night when the phone on the bar rang out loud and clear. He turned to answer it.

'Café Pacific. How may I help you?'

Down at the end of the table we heard a very businesslike Jean speaking calmly into her mobile phone.

'Hello. This is table six, over by the window. Could we have eight coffees, please? As quickly as possible.'

We drank a couple of toasts to Jean that night, the first in what was left of the house wine and then another, very thankfully, in hot coffee with cream.

CHAPTER EIGHT

We had had an early night for a change. For once I had managed to get Aileen into bed before the dawn chorus began to clear its throat for the day and I had slept like a log, although I suppose your average log doesn't wake up in a wild panic at a quarter past four in the morning and then squat on the bathroom floor for half an hour, smoking a cigarette and sweating profusely as it tries to remember what it was it should be worrying about.

Most nights I crawl into bed and drop off to sleep the moment my head touches the pillow. Then, in the early hours, the first shaft of light creeps into the bedroom and pokes at me with a bony finger.

'Wake up.'

Something truly terrible must have happened. I never quite know what it is but I should have been prepared.

'That's your trouble – you just don't think.'

Is it Aileen, is it the kids? Whatever it is it must be my fault. I should have known this was going to happen. If only...

And then I'm squatting stark naked on the bathroom carpet once again, worried sick and trying to make some sense of it all.

Last night I had been there – done that. But now I had calmed down, cooled off and was cosily curled up under the duvet once again, floating about in an altogether far more pleasant land in which I have been known to strike the winning goal at Wembley, score a century at Lords and scoop the National Lottery, all in a rollover week.

And then the phone rang.

I am very impressive when woken by natural forces – you would have been proud of me. Within seconds I was on my feet, phone in hand, speaking in dark brown, measured, masculine tones. I would have answered with my name had I been able to remember it. However, it wasn't important.

'Hello?'

It was my gorgeous daughter-in-law Lisa ringing from the south of France. She and Nick had called only last night to tell us the good news. They had found a site in Nice on which to open a second restaurant.

They already owned the *Countess of Evesham*, a delightful river boat moored by the Shakespeare Theatre in Stratford-upon-Avon, which serves both wonderful food and mouth-watering scenery as it cruises up and down the river twice a day. Now they wanted to spread their wings and take on another challenge. They had combed the likes of

Norwich and Cambridge on the lookout for suitable sites before realizing that, courtesy of easyJet, the south of France was almost on their doorstep.

Last night they had bought a run-down billiard hall and bistro on the rue Alphonse Karr in Nice and they were planning to convert it into the restaurant of their dreams. They were out on the town celebrating when they rang and our conversation had been punctuated with the sounds of laughter and the popping of champagne corks.

This morning, however, the call was far more brisk and businesslike.

'Sorry to get you out of bed. Would you ring directory enquiries for me? I need the number of our insurance company.'

'Of course.'

Still on automatic pilot I raced downstairs and carefully called directory enquiries. All hell was let loose.

On reflection I think the burglar alarm must have been as surprised as I was. It didn't half go on about it. To be honest I think it made a bit of a meal of it, but at least it woke me up.

Eventually I came across a phone which happened to be sitting on my desk at the time and passed on the relevant information to a very patient Lisa.

'Thanks.'

'No trouble. What's the problem?'

110

'Some idiots have broken into the *Countess* and set her on fire.'

It wasn't until much later that day that I heard the whole story. At the same time as Nick and Lisa were celebrating their expansion into Europe, three yobboes aged between fourteen and nineteen had forced their way into the boat at Stratford, stolen a miserable three bottles of wine and then started a fire in the kitchen to destroy any evidence.

At least they didn't take much catching. The police had an idea who they might be and as luck would have it a customer had inadvertently left his mobile phone on the table after finishing his meal and the thieves had taken it with them as an afterthought. A young waiter had put it to one side and he remembered it well. The phone itself was nothing out of the ordinary, but it had been tucked into a leather case in the shape of Kermit the Frog.

When the police raided their house the teenagers had long since knocked back the three bottles of wine and already flogged the phone, but there on the sideboard sat good old Kermit, large as life, relishing his starring role as exhibit number one.

However, this was small recompense for the damage, the heartache and the hard work to come. The hallway and kitchen had been completely burnt out, and the wooden panelling in the dining room, together with the tables, chairs, wooden decking, carpets and curtains, was charred beyond redemption. Once the fire brigade had extinguished the blaze, the water damage had added the final touch. All for three bottles of wine and a bleeding frog.

I wondered how the kids would cope. The income from the *Countess of Evesham* was going to help finance the venture in Nice. For a brief hour or so they were the proud owners of a thriving business that had given birth to a promising young whippersnapper and now they were going to have to think long and hard about where they went from here.

They had worked themselves into the ground over the past few years, at first seven long days a week well into the early hours, overcoming every obstacle that had been thrown at them. It had involved hard physical graft as well as planning every minute detail until now the business ran like clockwork. Only a few weeks ago my ultra-feminine daughter-in-law had rung me about nothing in particular and I had asked what her plans were for that day.

'The boat's in dry dock and I'm going down to paint the hull with bitumen. What about you?'

'I'm ironing some linen table mats.'

The boat had become a member of the family. She slipped naturally into every conversation.

'How's the Countess?'

'She's not been too well.'

The engine had spluttered that day and gone on strike. I've had the same trouble with the car as I have tried to start her up in the garage and taken it in my stride, but then I didn't have a full complement of diners aboard charging their glasses and looking forward to a four-course meal and a pleasant cruise up the River Avon. It's not a problem that the owners of most restaurants have to cope with all that often.

More often than not, however, the dear old Countess had brought smiles to our faces.

One Monday morning in September nearly all the family had gathered together in London for Thora Hird's memorial service in Westminster Abbey.

Thora had happily touched all our lives at one time or another and the day was one of fond remembrance. From the very first moment, as the Salvation Army brass band marched boldly into the packed cathedral, belting out an extremely energetic rendition of 'Onward Christian Soldiers', it was a day of celebration of a very remarkable woman.

Greg Dyke, Victoria Wood and Alan Bennett paid tribute to Thora from the pulpit and her grandchildren Daisy and James Torme followed suit. Smiles and tears fought with each other for top billing, often one refusing to give way as the other arrived on stage. A full house and the audience wanting more – Thora would have loved it.

Afterwards Aileen and I had been invited by the BBC to a get-together of Thora's friends and family at a place on Broad Sanctuary, so all the kids went off to catch up on the latest news at a rather posh restaurant where we were to join them later.

I paused after I had guided Aileen through the glass swing doors and looked round the vast entrance hall to find out where we needed to be.

It didn't take long. Nothing so boring as a discreet sign slotted in the standard-issue hotel easel. Above the lift doors hung an enormous mural on which angels were gathered in heaven, lounging on fluffy white clouds as they gazed down to earth and watched as Dame Thora came up to join them – relaxed and smiling broadly as her trusty old Stannah stair lift carried her upwards and onwards through the clear blue skies.

By the time we rejoined our own family they had reached the coffee and mints stage and were in good voice. I didn't have to stop and look round this time as I pushed my way through yet another pair of glass doors.

I merely followed the trail of happy chatter to where all ten of them were gathered round a long table.

I noticed a gaggle of rather well-bred ladies tut-tutting nearby as we sat down.

'Oh, my God – there are more of them.'

Whenever a burst of laughter broke through to the surface I would glance across at the women and watch as their eyes spoke volumes.

'Young people these days.'

Lisa always carries a huge straw handbag with her, large enough to accommodate all the usual bits and pieces that a woman likes to have about her person, including a mobile phone, plus an enormous date-a-day volume that serves as an engagement diary for the boat. She takes restaurant bookings on the hoof.

She was sitting quietly at the end of the table making a note of the calls she had missed whilst the phone had been switched off in the Abbey. She'd ring them back later when the time was right. Then, as she reached out towards her coffee, the phone rang out loud and clear. The eyes glared across from the adjoining table, little pointed daggers heading in our direction.

'It really is too much.'

Lisa quietly answered the phone. 'The Countess of Evesham. How can I help you?'

The eyes somersaulted in their sockets

and then the heads locked together in a tight scrum. The Countess of Evesham, indeed – well, who would have thought it?

'Do you know – I had a feeling...'

'So did I.'

'You can always tell.'

The ladies who lunch caught me watching them and they turned and nodded and smiled most agreeably. For one brief moment I thought I might treat them to my special regal wave, but then thought better of it and decided to quit whilst we were ahead.

Life must go on. I took a shower, paying close attention to all my important little places, cleaned my teeth and went back into the bedroom to have a look at Aileen. She was snuggled up, out to the wide.

At first I couldn't find her. The word snuggled must have been originally coined to describe Aileen when she is tucked up in bed, fast asleep. She becomes a part of the mattress and she takes the pillow down there with her under the duvet where all three of them melt into one. Eventually I spotted the odd strawberry blond curl that had briefly come up for air and assumed that she must be in there somewhere.

Down in the kitchen the cats were wondering what the hell had taken me so long. I let them out of the front door – they like to check to see whether anything untoward has happened out there during the night. At one time they used to bound down the hall in front of me and then wait impatiently as I fiddled with the locks and bolts. Nowadays I have to wait for them as they toddle across the carpet like a couple of old biddies off to collect their pension. Once down the steps and out on the path they separate, Thermal to the right, Tigger to the left.

They each have their specific sniffing duties and I must admit they carry them out in an extremely thorough manner. Not a flower, not a bush is left unsniffed and when they return they sit together on the front step and compare notes.

I left them to it and went to fill up Nokia's dish on the back step. I pulled open the kitchen door and he fell inside.

'Sorry, Nokes.'

He picked himself up, dusted himself down and just as I was thinking that I really ought to take him in and look after him properly he took a mighty swipe at my foot and swaggered off to a safe distance, leaving three claw marks etched across the leather toe of my shoe.

I put on a pot of coffee, emptied the dishwasher and laid the table for breakfast. Then I stuck a couple of Persil tablets complete with their amazing fizzing action into a little string bag and chucked them deep into the bowels of the washing machine, cranked it up to number seven and switched it on. It's an exciting life being a writer.

When I went to see how our pair of highly trained sniffer cats were getting on Tigger was just strolling back up the path. She looked ridiculous. Bald as a coot on one side, she still walked with the air of a fashion model parading up the catwalk.

She sat down on the bottom step and waited for Thermal. His round always takes that bit longer. He has all the individual carnations to account for and he doesn't like to cut corners. So I told Tigger to give me a shout when they were ready to come in, went back to the kitchen and slipped two slices of brown bread into the toaster.

I love this time in the morning. A couple of slices of toast topped with just the merest suggestion of Silver Shred, a pot full of hot coffee and the *Daily Telegraph* spread out on the table in front of me. I read quietly to myself, at the same time making a mental note of the articles and bits and pieces I would read out loud to Aileen later in the morning.

I get very angry every now and then with the paper's one-sided approach to politics and some of the rather precious articles by some of its rather precious columnists make my blood boil, but others are excellent and life wouldn't be the same without its sports section, its cryptic crossword and above all its page of reader's letters. Aileen will love this one.

Over the past week or so, various doctors had written in to say that they were experiencing considerable difficulties in understanding their immigrant patients as they attempted to describe their symptoms. Then a number of patients joined in the debate, adding that they had problems in understanding exactly what their foreign doctors were trying to tell them.

Today a vet seemed to have wrapped up the whole matter by writing to say that the problem wasn't confined to dealing with immigrants. He was from the home counties and his initial appointment, after he had qualified, was with a practice tucked away in a small village up in North Yorkshire.

On his very first day, his very first patient marched into his surgery with a rather embarrassed-looking Jack Russell terrier tucked under his arm and totally flummoxed him by announcing, 'Eeeh oop, mi duck – it's mi dog. It's got 'trots.'

That afternoon I walked up to Marsh to have my hair cut. I had my mobile phone with me in case Nick or Lisa rang. They would be back from France by now and have taken a good look at the damage on the boat and I wanted to know what they had decided. Would they be able to bring the dear old Countess back into the land of the living or would they have to switch off her life support system?

I had to pop into the bank before I went to have my locks trimmed and titivated. It's a very small, but very busy, branch of HSBC and we wouldn't be without it. There's nearly always a queue and today it had taken on the shape of a Danish pastry. The end was somewhere in the middle and it took a bit of finding. Eventually I located it by shouting, 'Where's the end?'

A woman raised her hand and I went and stood behind her. My bum was only about six inches away from the cashier's window but I would have to complete three circuits of the building before I eventually approached it from the right direction.

I had three hundred and fifty pounds in cash, which makes a nice change for me. My fees and advances are usually paid straight into the bank without my being able to touch them, stroke them or bounce them up and down on my knee.

The woman in front of me was becoming rather agitated. The queue seemed to have ground to a halt. At the window behind us the owner of a local Indian take-away was banking the week's takings, which he had tucked away in secret locations all about his person. The cashier had told him he was fifty-three pounds short and he was searching for it in a manner which would have had him arrested had he been caught doing it out on the street.

At the other window a rather sweet old lady was cashing in what seemed to be a lifetime's collection of two-pence pieces which she had filed away in dozens of empty Smartie tubes.

The woman in front of me finally cracked.

'I can't wait any longer. My daughter'll be out of school any minute now and I only want to cash a cheque for twenty pounds.'

I heard a voice I recognized from somewhere chime up, 'Never mind, love. I'll cash it for you.'

It only dawned on me that it was me who had just said that when the woman pressed a cheque into my hand and thanked me profusely.

'Not at all.'

I gave her a twenty-pound note and she was still trying to work her way out of the scrum when another woman leaned over from one of the outer layers of the pastry and poked my arm.

'You couldn't manage twenty-five, could you?'

I sorted her out and then a man who had almost reached the finishing line, lying in third place, just behind the rather sweet old lady, watched in horror as she produced yet another batch of Smartie tubes from her plastic Co-op carrier bag. He turned and asked shyly, 'Would eighty-five be out of the question?'

I had no idea who he was but I'd seen him around and so we did a deal. Then, as the queue inched forwards, I slipped over to the little table with its biro on a chain to adjust my paying-in slip.

I wasn't really taking much of a chance cashing all these cheques. As I stood and totted them up I noticed that every one had been made out to Mr D. Longden. I had no idea that I was so well known. And at least I had cut the queue down by the odd place or two.

When I turned to rejoin it, I saw that it had closed up even more tightly than before. It also looked a bit longer. I couldn't remember which bit I'd popped out of earlier and there was no way they were going to allow me to elbow my way back in.

'Where's the end?'

A woman shot her hand up in the air and for the second time that afternoon I fastened myself onto the tail and waited.

I steeled myself as I pushed open the door of Hair By Trudy. They would have seen me coming as I negotiated the zebra crossing and they were ready for me.

'You're late.'

I tried to explain the delay in the bank but they weren't interested in excuses and Jenna yanked me upstairs before I was halfway through the story.

I love having my hair shampooed. Isn't it strange that when you wash your hair at home you can barely feel the impact of your own fingers as they work their way round your scalp, and yet when someone who knows what they are doing takes over the task, it's the most relaxing and wondrous of experiences.

It always makes me feel a foot taller, but then Trudy cuts me down to size as soon as I approach the chair.

'Have you been snipping at this yourself?'

'No, I have not.'

'Mmmmm?'

I hadn't, but Trudy has a whole armoury of 'Mmmmm's. This was one of those deadly 'Mmmmm's that immediately defeat any attempt at a comeback, the sort of 'Mmmmm' that always makes me wonder if I've been snipping at it myself without realizing it.

It's a good job I love her. She's a true artist with the scissors, but today she was fully booked and had to hand me over to Sharon.

Sharon has the most beautiful face. Europe and the West Indies melt into a gentle fusion of peace and calm and whenever she smiles the whole place lights up.

She also has a wonderful way with words. She once told me that her mum and dad were thinking of moving back to Grenada. 'They get a better climax over there.'

Right on cue her mother popped her head round the salon door.

'That blanket I'm knitting for the cocka-teel's cage – do you want it to match the kitchen?'

Sharon thought that would be a great idea.

'Yes. Purple would be nice.'

You can see where she gets it from.

As she gradually turned me back into something that vaguely resembled a human being I began to feel rather drowsy, and a yawn that had been teetering on the edge for some time now suddenly broke loose and almost turned my face inside out.

'Sorry.'

''S all right. You see, I can't yawn when I'm working on a customer because they'd see me in the mirror and think I was bored, so I've learned to yawn through my eyes.'

I spent the remainder of my half hour trying to yawn through my eyes but I still have a long way to go.

Sharon stood back and admired her handiwork, then gave me a quick tour round the back of my head with a hand-held mirror and I was all done and dusted.

A young man who had never once taken his eyes off Sharon as she tried to make me look something like, eagerly slipped into my chair.

She ran her fingers through his long hair. 'What do you do then?'

'I'm at the university.'

'What are you studying?'

'Economics.'

'Oh.' She set to work with the scissors. 'What's that all about then?'✗

I took a slight detour through the park on the way home. An Alsatian I'd often seen from my office window was trotting ahead of me and that's the way he went so that's the way I went.

He often comes down from Marsh on his own. He brings his tennis ball with him and asks people to throw it for him. I sat down on a bench and he came over and dropped it at my feet.

I threw it for him and he bounded off after it and brought it back. We did this a dozen or so times and I was just wondering how on earth I was going to get away without hurting his feelings when my phone went off in my pocket.

It was Nick.

'Hi, Dad. I knew you must be worrying. We've just had a look at the boat and it's a nightmare. It's even worse than we imagined, but we've had some people in to have a look at her and we are going to rebuild her. When we've finished she'll be even more beautiful than before.'

I jumped to my feet and ran all the way home to tell Aileen. Behind me the Alsatian sat down on the path with a frown on his face and tried to work out what it was that he could have said to offend me.

CHAPTER NINE

I was out in the garden practising sitting very still when the phone rang. A most elegant blackbird was taking a bath in the little pond and I didn't want to disturb him, even though my coffee was growing colder by the second.

He had already seen off a bunch of unruly starlings who had tried to muscle in and take over the fishing rights. He was out-numbered on all sides, but it didn't take him long to sort them out and send them packing.

'All right, mate, all right – have it your way. Nice beak.'

He was concentrating very hard on his important little places when the telephone rudely interrupted his ablutions. He glared at me and then noisily shot away over the wall before I could apologize and explain that it wasn't me who had set it off.

'Hello.'

'Eeeh oop, mi duck – it's Mick.'

I've known Mick Peat for longer than I care to remember. We used to work together at BBC Radio Derby. His was the station's voice of authority on folk and country music and I did anything that might earn me a bob or two.

We didn't meet up for a number of years and then one day he happened to be in the audience as I was earning a crust on the cavernous stage of the Winding Wheel theatre in Chesterfield.

After the show was all done and dusted we had a drink together. I was wearing a new blue jacket and looked incredibly smart. He wasn't and didn't.

'What did you think?'

Mick took a pull on his pint. 'Who arranges these things?'

'I do.'

'Thought so.'

'How do you mean?'

'You can't watch yourself from out front. You didn't have the curtains closed and we could see that vast empty space stretched out behind you. You looked just like a tom-tit on a shovel.'

Mick now acts as an agent for me and organizes the events so that I can concentrate on simply doing my job, and he had arranged for me to talk in his home village of Crich in Derbyshire.

'Can you give me the post code of the venue, Mick, so I can punch it into my satellite navigation system?'

He thought about it for a second or so, but he can't really be doing with such nonsense.

'You know your way to Crich, don't you?'

'Yes, but I don't know where I'm talking once I get there.'

His directions were short and to the point.

'Well – when you get into 'centre of 'village, just stand wi' your back to 'chip shop and look uphill.'

I did and it worked wonderfully.

I tucked myself away in my office and wrote for the rest of the morning. It's difficult to write about writing. It's an extremely boring spectator sport, a bit like American football in that nothing happens for most of the time.

I was miles away, staring at the screen, lost to the world, when Aileen put her head round the door.

'Are you in here?'

'Yes.'

'Where?'

'Sorry, love. At my desk.'

She came over and handed me the phone.

'Who is it?'

'It's a rather thin lady, about forty.'

I dealt with the call and then went downstairs to rustle up some lunch for the two of us.

'How did you know she was thin?'

'She had a very slim voice.'

129

There are things in this world of which I know nothing.

That afternoon I had to pop over to Leeds for a radio interview. They ring me every now and then when they can't get anyone else, or someone much more important than me has let them down. I'm not too far away and I'm at home most of the time, so I am very handy to have around.

Three of us were to be on the programme. One was a man who had fallen in love with his dog, but the powers that be wouldn't let him marry it so he was preparing to appeal to the European Court of Human Rights. I found that the two of us didn't have all that much in common. The other was a lovely old lady who just happened to be a hundred and two years old that very day. We were all gathered together in the hospitality suite, which is basically a settee in a corridor.

A young woman with a clipboard in her hand came to take a few notes prior to letting us loose on the presenter and out of courtesy she started with the old lady.

'Tell me – the day you reached a hundred, did you feel really old?'

The lady thought about it.

'No,' she said. 'No I didn't – but I do now.'

'Why's that?'

'They've just put my youngest daughter into an old folk's home.'

I thought about that on the way home. I remembered visiting my own mother as she saw out her final days in a home for the bewildered. She couldn't even string a couple of words together and had absolutely no idea who I was.

By the end of visiting time she had more or less worked out that I was somehow loosely related to her and cried when I had to leave.

I remembered how some of the conversations went.

'When – did – you – have – them – last – Mum?'

No matter how many dashes I employed in order to slow down the flow of the sentence, she would simply stare at me blankly. In the end I would have to search under her pillows, under her sheets and under her bed, even deep down inside her nightdress, in pursuit of her runaway teeth.

The thought of her having to do the same for me in such circumstances doesn't bear thinking about. My mother once told me, many years ago, 'If you don't keep a close eye on life it has a very bad habit of coming at you backwards road on.'

I had no idea what she was on about at the time and it still doesn't make all that much sense to me, but I suppose having your youngest daughter put into an old folk's home is about as near as it gets.

When I got home Nokia raced excitedly down the path to greet me. Had he been a dog his tail would have been going like the clappers.

'It's my mate – he's back.'

Then, all of a sudden, for no reason whatsoever, he slammed on the brakes and went and hid behind a convenient bush. He desperately wants to become a part of the family but has absolutely no idea how to go about it.

I knelt down and had a somewhat one-sided conversation with him under the bush, and then carried on through the tall gate into the courtyard. I had intended to take my mobile phone with me to Leeds but had left it sitting on the little iron table after Mick had called earlier.

Nokia came out of hiding and trotted along at a safe distance behind me until he saw me stop dead in my tracks, at which point he panicked once again and immediately sought out the cover of yet another convenient bush. I had braked sharply because across the courtyard, just outside the back door, helping himself from Nokia's bowl of nourishing dry cat food was the grey squirrel from the park, stuffing his cheeks so full of the hard little biscuity things that he now looked as though he had a couple of furry saddlebags slung over the top of his head.

Just above him, perched on the roof of Nokia's kennel, sat the big black crow whom I had last seen helping the squirrel finish off the bag of fish and chips across the road. It seemed that they had now teamed up as a double act and were scavenging in tandem.

As soon as they saw me they were off, which rather surprised Nokia who hadn't known they were there in the first place. The crow cleared his head by a mere few inches and the squirrel almost barged him out of the way. All this excitement was far too much for a cat of such a nervous disposition. He scurried over to his kennel and settled down with his head butted up against the far wall and his big black bum stuck across the doorway in a vain attempt to shut out a most confusing world.

I picked up my phone and wandered slowly back through the garden. So many flowers still wearing their best bib and tucker even at this time of the year and I'd be damned if I could remember the names of any of them.

Aileen often puts me right over breakfast and then by lunchtime I've completely forgotten every word she said, so I make up my own names for them and my more knowledgeable friends then put me right the moment I open my mouth. My less horticulturally aware acquaintances, however, recognize me as a true son of the soil and hang on to every word I say.

Right opposite the front door we have a wonderful display of flowering Equilibrium. You should have seen it a couple of months ago, it was simply a riot of colour.

Down by the side of the front gate – no, not that side, the other side, the side opposite the hedge, that's it – is the most fantastic bed of early blooming Syphilis you will ever see in your life. It's a perennial, of course, and spreads like mad if you're not careful, so always make sure you are wearing rubber gloves and a balaclava.

Weaving its way intricately in and out of the trellis work on the back wall is a fine example of that beautiful old climber Impending Diphtheria, its fragrant lilac-blue flowers a concentrated mass of – well, I suppose you would call it lilac and blue really.

Actually the only plant that I instantly recognize whenever I come across it is the good old Busy Lizzie, the working class hero of the flower world. An absolute trouper with no pretensions whatsoever – it just gets on with the job in hand and is absolutely sure of its place in the grand scheme of things. I have always tried to model myself on the Busy Lizzie.

I had a quiet peep into Aileen's study in case she was in the middle of chatting up her computer, but she was fast asleep on the settee, out like a light, all snuggled up cosily under one of those fur throws that are all the rage these days.

She bought four of them in August while they were on special offer on the shopping channel and has spread them all round the house so that she's never very far away from an instant fur-lined nap.

I thought it seemed a bit like overkill at the time.

'It's as warm as toast outside.'

'Yes. But you just wait until the comforting warmth of August has given way to the bitter coldth of September. Then you'll be glad of them.'

She's fluent in four languages. German, French, Latin and Free Range English.

I switched on my computer and left it to its own devices as it heated itself up to gas mark seven, or whatever it is that these things do. I really don't need to know; it always gives me a shout when it's ready.

I stood by the window and looked out over the park. On a bench down below me a young couple snuggled up close together, each feeding the other from a plastic take-away dish of noodles and whatever. The back of the man's spare hand gently caressed the nape of the girl's neck as her long fingers twisted their way in and out through his unruly mop of hair. As she tilted her head back onto his shoulder and he spoon-fed her yet another helping of love and hot noodles, I became very much aware that the scene below me was becoming more erotic by the second and the voices inside my head began to have their say.

'You shouldn't be watching this – it's private.'

'Don't be ridiculous. What do you think he pays his council tax for?'

At that moment an ancient blue Volvo estate car spluttered up the road and juddered to an arthritic halt, pulling up right between me and the two lovers, hiding them from view.

'Bugger!'

'Serves you right.'

Nothing seemed to happen for some time, but then from my elevated position I could see that the aged driver of the Volvo was attempting to work out how to free the little metal bit at one end of his seat belt from the little metal bit at the other end of his seat belt, the little metal bit that is clamped securely to the floor.

His lady passenger appeared to be offering a constant stream of advice on the subject and it didn't seem to be helping him one little bit.

Eventually he achieved lift-off and decided

to take a few minutes' rest before winding his window right up to the top three times to make sure it was properly shut and then testing at length to see that his handbrake was indeed well and truly engaged.

It must have been ten minutes or so before the driver's door began to ease open and a brown-trousered leg appeared, followed by a brown bum of immense proportions and then another leg, which seemed to be rather similar in size and colour to the first.

He bent and took a duffle coat from the rear seat and then spent a fair old time fiddling around with his loops and toggles before shuffling round the bonnet to assist his good lady from the car.

It was clear now that he found it impossible to stand with his back anywhere near straight. He was bent almost double so that he was forever staring down at his knees, which came in very handy when he stopped for a brief moment to rub his headlights with his left sleeve but must be one hell of a handicap when it came to dealing with most other things in life.

He tugged open the passenger door and helped his wife out onto the pavement before wrapping her up in a matching duffle coat. She thanked him sweetly and together they went round to the back of the car and opened the rear doors.

She dealt with all the locks and catches

above the waist, he dealt with those below, and between them they dragged from the car a thin plank, which they eventually manhandled into position as some sort of ramp. Then they each stood guard, one on either side, as the oldest sheepdog in the world waddled slowly out of the back of the estate car and on down the slope towards the road below.

The young couple, their arms still wrapped round each other, came trotting up the park steps and then stood on the pavement and watched as the frail old dog finally negotiated a safe touchdown onto the tarmac.

The girl disentangled herself and ran forward, knelt down on one knee, put both arms round the dog's neck and rubbed her head against his cheek. Mother Nature had already decreed that the old man's head would come along at any moment and join the pair of them down there, and as the three of them chatted to one another the young man helped the old lady pack the plank back into the car and lock up.

The dog didn't seem to have all that much to say for itself. At one point I thought he was about to wag his tail, but then, after jacking it up half a turn into a horizontal position, he must have decided that this was going to take far too much effort to be worth it and the tail just stayed up there in mid-air, like a ready primed pump handle.

At this point in the proceedings I desperately needed to go to the lavatory. I had been putting it off for much longer than was sensible and so I raced off and then raced back again in almost no time whatsoever. (I washed my hands, honest. Both of them.)

I was back just in time to see the old couple negotiate the three steps down into the park. Talk about teamwork. He looked after her, she looked after him, they both looked after the dog and the dog was determined to be as little trouble as possible.

The youngsters were watching their every move from up there on the pavement, the girl itching to pitch in and help, but the three ancient ones had been through all this many times before. The dog waited as the two humans slowly lowered themselves down onto the bench the two youngsters had vacated only a few minutes earlier. It would still be warm.

On sitting down, the old man's back became as straight as a ramrod and for a brief few moments he would tower above his wife. She smiled up at him and stroked his thigh. The two then reached over and shuffled the dog along a bit. His back legs seemed to have seized up and he needed a jump start and a bit of a lift to get him going.

He eventually collapsed across their ankles, trapping their feet under a mountain of flesh and a whole lot of fur. He could drop off in peace now. They wouldn't be going anywhere without him knowing about it.

The old man caressed the nape of his wife's neck with the back of his hand and then popped a boiled sweet in between her open lips. She kissed his cheek and laid her head on his shoulders, her long fingers reaching out and stroking a scalp that once must have been home to a fine head of hair.

The youngsters strolled off, hand in hand, wrapped up in the warmth of their own thoughts and full of the excitement of young love.

In fifty years' time it could be the two of them sitting on that very same bench, lovingly holding hands and still desperately needing one another after all those years.

If they were very, very lucky.

CHAPTER TEN

The doorbell rang twice, very loudly. Our back doorbell is just over one hundred years old, it's made of solid brass and is about ten centimetres across. They knew how to make doorbells in those days. Aileen paused over her coffee.

'I wonder who that is?'

'The postman.'

'How do you know?'

'Must be. *The Postman Always Rings Twice*.'

'Does he?'

'No, not necessarily. It was the title of a film. Jack Nicholson was in it. *The Postman Always Rings Twice*.'

The doorbell rang again. Twice.

'Hadn't you better answer it?'

'I suppose I better had.'

It was the postman.

Not the usual postman. This was the other postman, the one who drives a van and specializes in parcels. Doesn't talk much.

'Sign here.'

I signed there and then took the odd shaped package into the kitchen so that Aileen could run her hands over it.

141

'It's for you, love – it's from QVC.'

She ran her hands over it. 'I think it's for you.'

'For me?'

She gave me a great big smile. 'It's a present – from me.'

'Oh. Really, you shouldn't have.'

Now when most people tell a loved one that they really shouldn't have, that often isn't what they mean at all. It's merely another piece of social shorthand for a whole rack of emotions ranging from: 'How sweet of you to have remembered' to: 'You would have been found dead in a ditch if you hadn't.' But whenever I say to Aileen: 'Really, you shouldn't have', nine times out of ten that is exactly what I mean.

She worries that I have to do all the cooking, a lot of the cleaning and the hundred and one other little jobs that come along with the honour of being appointed as her official guide dog.

She shouldn't. I really don't know what I would do without her. She's a walking Encyclopedia Britannica, wonderful company, a most enthusiastic lover, she makes me laugh a lot and she is one of the few people who can't see how much I have aged over these past few years.

But then she will keep trying to ease my burden by buying me the latest gadget that has recently appeared on one of the television shopping channels.

Some of them have been wonderful. The baking sheets made out of some sort of rubber stuff are fantastic and save me hours of Brillo-pad wielding; the omelette maker is a pleasure to use and easy to clean. The winged frying pan has simply changed my life and the Lock & Lock plastic containers have turned my disorganized fridge into a thing of beauty.

It's the awkward brigade that I find so frustrating. The expensive juicer that within half an hour had crusted over with an unremovable coating of orange and lemon gunge. The chip fryer from hell and the polythene bag sealer that was on a work experience scheme and didn't fancy the experience. The electric pepper mill that panicked the moment it had to deal with its very first peppercorn. The bread-making machine that bounced all over the kitchen before eventually giving birth to a small wet loaf that had a mixing paddle stuck up its backside. That one small loaf cost Aileen a cool £98.25, plus £4.95 package and postage, and it wasn't even sliced.

Today's mystery gift looked the strangest of the lot.

'Have you guessed what it is yet?'

I wouldn't have guessed in a million years, but since I now had it already unpacked and laid out on the kitchen table I could make a pretty shrewd stab at it.

'It's a mop and a bucket.'

'It's the very latest in mops and buckets.'

You could tell it was. It came with a book of instructions. I read through them twice and I couldn't make head or tail of them.

'It seems quite complicated for a mop and bucket.'

'It cuts cleaning time in half.'

'It's very nice, love. Thank you very much.'

'Try it out.'

I tried but I couldn't find out how to extend the mop handle. It had a technically advanced locking system that had me beaten all ends up and the bucket had a special filling system together with a revolutionary sloped bottom which was there to facilitate something or other, but I never found out what it was.

I was saved by the bell. The door bell. Once again it rang twice and this time it was our regular postman who handed me a huge wad of letters.

This is Aileen's favourite time of the day. She always has a gut feeling that today there is going to be some really good news tucked away in one of those little sealed envelopes and so I poured her yet another cup of coffee and she settled down to hear what I had to say.

She has absolutely no privacy whatsoever. It would drive me mad, but over the years she has come to terms with it. First of all I read her bank statement out loud and we tried to work out why she should have sent a cheque for £48.37 to some firm in Reading of which she had never heard.

Then there was a lovely letter from an ardent fan in Harrogate and another from a builders' merchants informing her that the heated towel rails she enquired about are now in stock.

'I meant to tell you about those.'

There was a cheque from a firm of publishers who are reprinting a book that she wrote over thirty years ago, at which point I added a drop of brandy to her cup of coffee and a tot of whisky to my own.

Finally there was a Get Well Soon card from an old friend in Oswestry which puzzled us greatly since Aileen hasn't been at all unwell recently, isn't remotely unwell at the present time and has no intention of being unwell in the near future. Still, it was a nice thought.

I only had the one letter. From Sandra Chalmers, sister of Judith and an old friend of mine from my days on *Woman's Hour*. Some time ago she had asked me to write a monologue for Thora Hird on behalf of Help the Aged.

The charity had teamed up with British Gas to fight the devastating effects of cold on older people and now she was thanking me for having delivered on time. I may not be the best, but I usually deliver on time.

I remembered it well.

MONOLOGUE WRITTEN FOR DAME THORA HIRD – TO BE PERFORMED AT THE MAGIC CIRCLE THEATRE, LONDON

The room has a very cold feel about it. Dame Thora sits in a chair with a blanket round her, trying to keep warm. She has arthritis in her hands. Two copies of the Big Issue *sit on a small table by her side, with another copy resting on the arm of the chair.*

I didn't want to get up this morning. Oh, it was perishing. My net curtains were frozen to the window pane and there were them pretty fern patterns all over the glass.

I could see my breath when I said my prayers last night – they were like little smoke signals going up to heaven. *(Shivers)* Him up there'll think I'm a Red Indian if I'm not careful.

I'm supposed to be booked into Old Brampton when I go. We've got a double plot so as I can join my Leslie.

The way I'm going I could finish up in some happy hunting ground somewhere or other.

She takes a perfume spray and squirts a little down the top of her dress.

146

I only had a stand-up wash this morning. The water were like ice, so I skimped a bit. I went as far down as possible and as far up as needs be and that were that. I'm getting very idle.

I think I might sleep down here tonight. It's very damp in that bed. It didn't used to be – not when Leslie was alive. He always switched the fan heater on an hour before we went upstairs and then we'd snuggle up together.

Can't afford to do that now. I only just managed to scrape the heating bill together last quarter and that was for the summer months. They'll cut me off if I'm not careful and then where will I be?

They can take your house off you, can't they?

She adjusts the blanket and tries to ease the arthritis in her hands.

It's not nice when you first get into bed. The damp's got a hold on the mattress now and it's like sleeping on a pudding – a cold rice pudding – and then when you wake up in the morning you think you're sweating, but you're not. It's just that the damp's warmed up a bit and gone all squishy.

I hate the damp. It feels dirty.

I sometimes think my bones have gone damp.

Looks around.

I wonder where the cat is. I could do with

him now. He jumps up and sits on my knee and I can feel the heat from his little body. Then when he's asleep I move him around – up on my bust and down round my thighs. He never knows anything about it. Once he's dropped off he's out like a light. He's better than a hot water bottle.

You don't have to keep topping him up.

I tuck my hands in underneath him and rub his tummy. It helps with this toothache I've got in my fingers.

Mind you, he's riddled with arthritis himself. Whenever you stroke him you can feel the knots in his little thighs up at the back end. All knobbly.

Fancy having arthritis when you're only thirteen years old. You see, there's always somebody worse off than yourself.

I hope he hasn't caught it off me.

She rubs her hands again and nods to a point across the room.

There's condensation running down that wall. It wouldn't have dared do that when Leslie was alive.

Pauses to look around once more.

Puss! Puss!

He's probably nipped round next door. They've quite taken to him. Mrs Singh says he sits on their boiler and watches them while they have their tea. She said did I mind him going round there – I said no of course I didn't. *(Shivers)* I could do with him now though.

I wish I could go round and sit on their boiler.

Checks her watch.

I'm going to switch the fire on in – *(checks her watch again)* in twenty-seven minutes. Just for half an hour or so. It's my little treat for today.

It looks nothing now – you can tell those logs are artificial – but once it gets itself under way it looks lovely and there's all flames licking up at the back and you'd swear they were the real thing.

Leslie and me used to have to push our chairs back.

Only you see these days I'm frightened of falling asleep while it's on. I do that a lot nowadays. Last week I nodded off and then when I woke up it had been on for three and a half hours. God knows what that'll cost me.

So I haven't had it on since.

Checks her watch once more.

Twenty-six minutes.

They're a nice family, the Singhs. She comes round every now and then to see how I am. She doesn't stop long. I think it's too cold for her.

Well, it's hot where she comes from, isn't it? And she only wears sandals and that sari thing with a cardigan over the top. Mind you, I don't know what she's got on underneath.

149

I've got three vests on. Two of mine and one of Leslie's. It's called layering, you see, and that way you build up little pockets of warm air between each vest and it keeps you a lot warmer in the winter. My mother taught me that.

Only it doesn't seem quite as effective these days. Perhaps my vests are on the blink. I'll have to switch 'em round. *(Pause)* I'm feeling drowsy.

Nods to indicate next door.

He must have a good job. They've got central heating and double glazing and they've just had the roof isolated.

Leslie was going to have our roof isolated but he never got round to it. Doesn't really matter now.

I couldn't afford to switch it on.

It's funny. I get sixty-eight pounds a week with my pension and it's a lot of money, isn't it? And then they gave me an extra twenty-five pence a week just because I was eighty. You'd think I'd be able to manage, but it doesn't seem to go anywhere.

With me it's either heating or eating and you've got to eat to stay alive, haven't you?

Mr Singh says he's sure there is something I could claim for and would I like him to ask around for me, but I told him no. Me and my Leslie never claimed for anything.

Leslie always said that once they had you on their list then they'd got you where they wanted you. They could have me out of here and into a home like a shot and I don't want to leave here.

I know everyone round here. *(Pause)* No I don't. Not any more. Just Mrs Godber and the Singhs.

Checks her watch again.

I used to go round to the library and have a warm-up there, but they've started shutting it down three days a week and I can never remember when it's open – and it's a long trek up there if they've put the latch on.

Most places if you hang around you've got to start buying things. I sometimes sit on that bench at the far end of the mall. It's all covered in, you see, like a big greenhouse, and it's ever so warm – although I could do without that water feature.

It always makes me want to go does that.

There's a young man stands opposite. I bought a magazine off him. *(Picks up the magazine from the arm of the chair and reads)* The *Big Issue*.

His dog looked like it could do with a square meal. Eighty pence he said it was. He said he hadn't got any change so I said to give it to the dog and he said he would and it were money well spent if he did. *(She pats the magazines on the table)* I've bought three off him this month, but you can still see its little ribs sticking out. *(She drops the magazine on top of the other two on the table with a sniff and a shake of the head)* There's not a lot in it for me.

I must be daft. I could do with that money now. I've run out until pension day and this'll be two weeks running I've missed my television stamp. It'll have to be beans on toast again.

Still they're very nutritious aren't they? And they're very handy – you only have to use the one ring on the cooker, you see. Saves on the gas.

Realizes.

Oh no. I've run out of bread. Suppose it'll have to be beans on beans again.

I don't know what I'm going to do about the television. I should miss it. It's like having friends round to visit – but it's over a hundred pounds a year, that licence, you know.

Mrs Godber down the road pays hers all in one go because if she does then she gets one pound twenty-five pence a year knocked off.

That's a special concession because she's blind.

I don't think it's much of a bargain, that.

So I buy the stamps myself – but I'm always falling behind. *(She glances at the pile of magazines)* I shouldn't have bought 'em, should I? But he had such a sad little face and he wagged his tail when I patted him.

152

I can feel *my* ribs – even through this lot. No wonder I'm freezing. There's not a lot on me these days. *(Checks her watch)* Nineteen minutes and I'll switch it on.

She pulls the blanket up round her.

I think this blanket's getting thinner. I'm sure it used to be warmer than this. Mrs Singh says I should get myself one of those duvets but I've never been all that impressed.

They had one when I went to stay with our Vera in Eastbourne. Damn silly thing it was. I had to fiddle with a dozen or so buttons before I could get inside it. The next night I just slept with it on top of me and it was every bit as good.

She begins to settle down.

I think I'll have a little nap. Just a few minutes while I wait for the fire. I get very drowsy these days, even when it's cold.

I can't feel my feet. *(She feels her face)* I can't feel my face. It's just like Leslie's was after I shaved him and laid him out.

Bet *he's* feeling the cold. It's damp is that graveyard up at Old Brampton, always was.

Tries to make herself comfortable.

I wonder if he'd mind if I didn't join him. They'll only plonk me down on top of him. It's not as though we shall be able to hold hands, is it?

I wonder if he'd mind if I had myself cremated? *(As she drops off to sleep)* At least

I'd be warm for a change.
Fade.

When the night of the performance arrived I wondered how Thora was going to cope. We hadn't long been back from the Emmys ceremony in New York and Thora had seemed to be either on the radio or on television ever since, giving interview after interview.

Aileen and I drove down to London, both of us half baked and half asleep. We were absolutely knackered, but compared to Thora we were just a couple of kids. Thora was now in her late eighties and she had been through much the same schedule, having had little or no time to learn the monologue, never mind rehearse it.

When she arrived at the theatre she looked tired and pale and once on stage she seemed to have lost her usual air of confidence. She began reasonably well but I noticed that her pauses, which she always had timed down to the nanosecond, were just ever so slightly off.

Then she lost it. Completely forgot her words. But like the professional that she was she leaned over to the table and calmly picked up a script that she had hidden in one of the magazines.

She did it so well that nobody in the audience seemed to notice, apart from Aileen and me. We knew it wasn't in the script.

But then her eyes weren't up to it. She couldn't make out her lines and a prompter slipped out of the wings and settled down by the armchair. She took the script and quietly whispered the lead-in lines to Thora, who then gave them that wonderful twist of hers, polished over so many years – as though the words had just slipped into her head out of thin air.

She was incredible. Strangely enough, her general fragility and vulnerability brought home the point that Help the Aged were desperately trying to make and put it over in a far more graphic way than any script of mine could ever hope to achieve.

She graciously received her usual standing ovation and then Janette took her home and tucked her up in bed for a well-earned nap.

Aileen wanted to know if there was any more coffee in the pot and had I cracked the secret code of the dreaded mop and bucket.

I poured her another cup and topped it up with a generous shot of brandy. If I could get her stoned out of her mind she might forget all about it.

I read through the instructions yet again. I knew deep down that a ten-year-old child would have no trouble with them whatsoever, but I have the sort of mind that always throws up three or four possible alternatives. Do they mean this or do they mean that? I tie myself up in knots and in the end I have no idea what on earth they mean. Why is there never a ten-year-old child around when you need one?

Eventually Aileen became bored with hanging about and went up to her office to see if she had any e-mails on her computer.

I cleared the kitchen table into the dining area and set to work. On the instructions there was a photograph of a rather elegant woman in her best bib and tucker caressing the floor with a long-handled mop, and doing it with such ease and grace that you could tell the floor shone instantly and dried immediately and all was well with the world.

I still couldn't find out how to extend the handle and I was having a great deal of trouble removing the easi-fit lid from the top of the bucket, so I filled the sink, soaked the mop and got down on my hands and knees and scrubbed away at the floor like a madman.

Eventually it was reasonably clean but still soaking wet and so I dried it off with the hand towel by the side of the sink and then went over it again with a tea towel that just happened to be passing by.

Aileen was delighted that once again she had managed to make my life that bit easier.

'You were rather dubious at first, weren't you?'

I had to admit it. 'I was, yes. But you were right.'

She loves to be right. It gives her a warm glow all over.

CHAPTER ELEVEN

I had survived the horrors of the M6 during the teatime rush hour and then spent what seemed like a lifetime on that mysterious circle of motorways that surround Manchester at a time when they were being just plain silly.

Now at home I had to climb over a couple of ancient cats that had pinned themselves to the hall carpet and were unable to wave so much as a leg at me. I stepped over them, plonked my stack of books down by the hall cupboard and then went back to sort them out.

The trouble is that Thermal and Tigger hardly ever go anywhere these days, apart from their morning sniff around the flower beds, and they are not taking that little chore as seriously as in days gone by.

Struggling young flowers in their first flush of youth are feeling unwelcomed and un-sniffed; brave little bulbs are bravely break-ing through unnoticed and unloved; and unscheduled visits from the neighbourhood cats are going uncharted and unlogged.

One of the results of this ever increasing idleness is that the cats' claws are not being trimmed down by the stone pavers as God intended and they are becoming longer and more unmanageable by the hour.

Yesterday Thermal had to roll across the dining room carpet towards his supper dish, dragging his sheepskin rug along with him as he rolled. Once upon a time they would float silently as ghosts as they breathed into the kitchen, whereas these days they sound like a couple of naff Spanish dancers as they click-click-click their way across the lino. Now they had gone and got themselves stapled to the hall carpet.

The trouble with cats is that they won't be helped. It never seems to occur to them that all this is for their own good.

Why don't they think *'I'll just lie here quietly and let him get on with it'*? Or *'I've known him for seventeen years now and never once has he let me down'*?

No. They go berserk. They fight back and they scratch. One day I'm going to be really hard and let them lie there for as long as it takes for them to come to their senses.

In the meantime I half sat on them as I disentangled their claws and tried to ignore the swearing and cursing that was welling up from underneath my legs.

It took ages but eventually I managed to set them both free and they staggered off down to the comparative safety of the cellar, glaring back at me as they went.

'*Who the hell does he think he is?*'

There is a slight possibility that, rather than a dog, a cat might eventually turn out to be man's best friend, but it would never dream of admitting it.

I tidied up a small pile of claws that obviously hadn't been installed as well as they might have been in the first place and then went up the stairs to Aileen's office to see how her day had gone.

I don't just barge in. That would be rude. I listen at the door, which sounds just as rude but it isn't. If she's having a nap I don't want to disturb her. If she's talking to her computer I don't want to put her off. If she's talking on the phone then it's none of my business. She was talking on the phone so I put my ear to the door and listened in.

After a while I worked out that she was talking to Brian. He's the computer whizz kid who installed the Dragon Dictate and Jaws systems for her and now she was arranging for him to come over and give her a further half-day update. They get on very well, they have a lot in common. Brian is also blind.

They settled on the day and hour. He would get here on his own. Brian is very independent. Aileen signed off with a line that really touched me.

'Will we need eyes?'

Apparently Brian said that yes they would.

Of course I would be the eyes because I was always on hand. I would be needed, apparently, to stick a cable connection into one of those rows of honeycomb holes that punctuate the back of the computer. I could also make the coffee and sandwiches at lunchtime.

It seems so sad that two extraordinarily bright people such as Aileen and Brian couldn't complete a job without having a pillock like me around to take a plug and stick it in a hole for them. So sad.

I popped into my office to make a note. I keep a commonplace book in which I jot down little bits and pieces of conversation that appeal to me and today I had met a lovely old lady over at a golf club in Cheshire.

I was there to speak at a rather grand luncheon and before I go on show I always like a quiet few minutes to myself. I noticed a conservatory overlooking the golf course and hid myself away in there.

The view was absolutely fantastic. Rolling fairways, immaculately manicured greens and here and there a copse of trees. It seemed to go on for ever without a break, as far as the eye could see.

I didn't spot the old lady at first. She was sitting quietly down at the far end, in a wicker chair, her eyes glued to the wonderful view. I rehearsed the opening of my talk silently in my head and then it was time to join the others once more. As I passed by her chair, the woman was still in a world of her own, taking in the miles of glorious English countryside.

'Lovely, isn't it?'

She nodded absently. 'I can remember when all this was fields.'

It was such a surprising remark. My mother used to come up with it whenever we drove past a new housing development in Chesterfield, but here, stretching out as far as the horizon and probably beyond, it still was all fields.

She nodded towards the putting green. 'I was born right there. Lovely house. Been in the family for three hundred years.'

I settled my bum down on the window sill and listened as she painted me a word picture of this stretch of countryside as it was when she was a girl, furnishing it with two loving parents, a faithful old dog and her first boyfriend, whom she should have married but didn't.

She touched on the war. The proper war, not this latest one. This latest one was when things started to fall apart. Her father was killed; her brother was an idle little devil and an idiot with money but her mother wouldn't hear a word against him.

They were just about to have the house sold right from under them when the chairman came looking for me.

'Two minutes, Mr Longden.'

Down on the putting green a golfer was settling over an eight-inch putt.

'That would have been our dining room.'

The putt missed by a mile and the golfer hurled his club at the turf in frustration. Thoughtless idiot – he'll ruin that carpet.

Later that evening I put a quick meal together. Steak and salad with a fresh fruit salad to follow. I'm not the greatest cook in the world; basically I just about keep the pair of us alive. More Little Chef than Gourmet Chef, but my salads are something else.

I'm at ease with a salad. For a start I can't burn a salad or leave it in the oven for too long. I have never yet had a salad boil over on me and I am always trying something different. Those so-called salads that creep shamefacedly out of the restaurant kitchen, three lettuce leaves, a couple of tomatoes and the odd slice of cucumber, where's the pride, where's the ingenuity?

I use only crisp lettuce hearts, cut as fine and as small as is humanly possible, tiny cubes of tomato, onion, cucumber, mush-room and bacon, maybe a boiled egg. Then I add sun-dried tomatoes, just a smidgen of pickled walnut and my cheese of the day, all chopped into minuscule chunks along with whatever happens to be in season. Sesame seeds and garlic help to bring the whole thing to life or sometimes the merest touch of lemon and lime. All you need then is a good Ranch dressing and we have lift-off.

'This is one I prepared earlier,' as a chef on television said the other day, whipping something or other out of the oven; 'all that we need to do now is to serve it along with a simple salad.'

Stuff that. My main course might be very simple – sometimes it can look as though it is positively retarded – but my salads are nothing short of great works of art.

My fruit salads are bought in, selected from Sainsbury's serve yourself section, the content of my plastic bowls constantly refined after long consultations with the woman who eats it all.

'The strawberries are beginning to go soft by the second day.'

Out went the strawberries.

'The watermelon tastes of nothing in particular.'

Out went the pink watermelon.

'The nuts and raisins are fine sprinkled throughout, but the dried banana goes all soft and squishy.'

The dried banana pieces now go on top where the assorted juices can't get at them.

All this market research has paid off in spades. Aileen loves her fruit salad and I love sitting across the table and watching her eat it. When she dips her spoon deep in her dish she has absolutely no idea what is going to come out of it on this occasion. As the spoon travels slowly up towards her mouth she frowns slightly, wondering exactly what she is going to taste in a couple of seconds. The mouth opens, the spoon slides in, her eyes ask the questions that her taste buds are quick to answer and then a smile of pure pleasure takes over centre stage.

Sometimes, like those toy cranes in the fairground, she misses and the spoon comes up with absolutely nothing on it at all. On those occasions she wipes the puzzled look from her face very quickly and pretends that it simply never happened.

It's pure theatre and a joy to watch and sometimes I am lucky enough to be able to fit in a matinée performance as well.

I switched on the television and chuntered away at it as I chopped up my salad. I've started talking to the television quite a lot recently. At least it never answers back – on the other hand it never takes a blind bit of notice of me either.

I wanted to find out this week's lottery numbers. Usually I wait until they are on teletext because I can't stand that long drawn out programme with the dumpy little Irishman.

Have you ever wondered why the lottery audience suddenly goes berserk when the number balls come spinning out of whatever it is they call that machine?

'First of all number two.'

The audience goes wild, cheering number two like mad. Who'd have thought it? Brave little number two – it's amazing when you think of the poor upbringing it had in the back streets of Salford. It could have been hooked on drink and drugs by now, but no – here it is, starring in a peak-time television programme and on a Saturday night at that. Let's hear it for number two.

I don't know what happens to the average human being once they become a member of a studio audience. I would think that hardly any of them has number two on their lottery ticket and yet off they go, wildly yelling their heads off.

'Number forty-seven.'

Off they go again, only this time a voice cuts across the hysterical multitude. A voice similar to the one I remember hearing on Pathé News some time in the late 1940s.

'This is the sixty-third time that number forty-seven has appeared since the first Saturday after Michaelmas the year before last.'

Who on earth gives a toss? All I want to know is whether or not I have won seven and a half million pounds, give or take a million or so.

I suppose I must be turning into a grumpy old man. Earlier in the week I had a shouting match with the gardening programme *Ground Force*, featuring Alan Titchmarsh and that lovely lady with the pair of splendidly independent breasts that have a completely separate life of their own. I can't remember her name offhand.

They were about to start work on an absolute bummer of a garden when the owner admitted that he hadn't bothered to do a damn thing with it for the past seven years. And now he wanted it tarting up as a surprise for his wife whose birthday it was and who would be back home from shopping with her sister in Birmingham around four o'clock that afternoon.

'Leave it, Alan,' I found myself yelling at the television. 'He's nothing but an idle little sod – he doesn't deserve you.'

But Alan took not the slightest bit of notice of me – he never does, not even when he can hear me. I've known him for over twenty years now and he's the loveliest man you could ever wish to meet, but he won't be told.

I shouted upstairs to let Aileen know that dinner was almost ready, but Thermal and Tigger beat her into the kitchen by a couple of short heads. They parked their bums expectantly by the fridge door and Aileen went over to the kitchen sink and began to wash the few bits and pieces that I had soaking in there.

'You leave it, love. I'll see to it.'

'It's OK – I've nearly finished.'

'Your dinner's on the table.'

'I won't be a minute.'

'The carving knife's in there. You could cut yourself.'

'Don't patronize me.'

'All right. You're a lousy washer-up and I'll only have to do it all over again when you're not looking.'

'That's more like it.'

And with that she dried her hands, pulled back her chair and sat down at the kitchen table.

I like Saturday nights. The week is all done and dusted and *Match of the Day* is but a few hours away. I had successfully fed Aileen and the cats and all three had seemed to be more than satisfied. Tigger jumped up on my knee and pounded and purred away whilst Thermal banged his head against my ankle and played silly devils with my shoelace. Aileen did none of these things, but then there was little or no room for her on my lap.

We hadn't had a chance to tackle the *Daily Telegraph* crossword today and every Saturday there is a prize on offer of a rather swish *Daily Telegraph* pen. Aileen has set her heart on being a winner one of these days, but I have a feeling that the envelopes we have been using up to now are far too shy and retiring. I need to find a brand-new sort of envelope that is openly brash and pushy, one who won't hesitate to force its way up to the top of the pile.

We had a go at the quick crossword first. It's a sort of warming-up exercise for her before she tackles the real thing.

'Try this one. Four letter word meaning to recognize.'

'No.'

'OK, we'll try another one.'

'No.'

'All right. Four letters – to recognize.'

'No.'

'Well what do you want to do then?'

'No. K-n-o-w. Know. To recognize.'

The phone burst into life and I had to leave the table to answer it. The phone is my friend and knows when I need to be rescued.

It was Nick on the other end of the line with some good news for a change. Ever since the vandals had set the *Countess of Evesham* on fire the other sort of news had been piling up thick and fast. Bureaucratic delays in Nice with the new restaurant – over here constant battles with the insurance company and the bank manager.

Now both the bank and the insurers had

come onside and were being fully supportive and Nick and Lisa were getting to grips with the weird and wonderful ways in which bureaucracy flourishes in France.

'The boat is looking absolutely beautiful. Just a few more weeks now, and Karrs is really beginning to take shape. Are you two going to pop over?'

I had already checked out the prices with easyJet. 'As soon as you open, but I'll need a special deal.'

'You've got it.'

'Great. OK if I bring the Tuesday Club along with me?'

'You always have to go and spoil everything, don't you?'

My granddaughter Katie was the next to check in. She wanted to thank me for her birthday present. I never know what to buy her on these occasions. I don't see her on a day-to-day basis and have no idea what the hip ten-year-old around Brighton is into these days so I send a cheque off to Sally and she does the rest.

'Thank you so much, Grampy. It was wonderful of you.'

'My pleasure, darling. So pleased you liked it.'

What on earth was it that Sally said that I had been generous enough to buy her this time?

'I love it. It was my very best present.'

What the hell was it?

'I think it was very clever of you to know that I desperately wanted a Gameboy.'

Ten years old and she's just as sarcastic as her mother. Where did I go wrong?

At least my kids have the common sense not to ring up whilst *Match of the Day* is in progress, but Aileen's lot just don't seem to think. I feel that it says a lot about the way they were brought up.

Aileen doesn't seem to mind, either. It's a funny old world. Annie was the first on the line. She and Martyn have bought this wonderful old place in the Royal Crescent in Bath. It has rooms you can get lost in. I always feel that Aileen and I ought to be roped together as we leave the guest bedroom first thing in the morning and then go on safari in an attempt to find the kitchen. I always make sure I have my mobile phone with me just in case.

David was next. I'm surprised he took the trouble. He had called earlier in the week.

'Hi, Deric - can I just have a quick word with my mum?'

'Course you can. How's Lubka?'

'She's fine.'

'Give her my love. Won't be a minute.'

I took the phone into the lounge. 'Aileen – it's David on the phone.'

She had her forehead pressed up against the television screen. 'Tell him to ring back after *Casualty.*'

I took the phone out into the hall. 'Sorry, David – she's rather busy at the moment. She says would you mind ringing back in about half an hour?'

'Course I will. What is it – have I hit *Casualty* again?'

The adverts were on when I went back into the lounge and so I was allowed to speak to her.

'I don't know – what sort of a mother are you?'

She didn't bat an eyelid.

'Totally unnatural,' she said. 'Totally un-natural.'

CHAPTER TWELVE

The post is getting later these days. It was just after half past twelve when I heard the dull thud of junk mail bouncing on the hall carpet. I can remember a time when it was here long before I left for work and then we had another delivery round about lunchtime. Good grief. I'm sounding really ancient – give me another six months and I shall be remembering when all this was fields.

So what have we here? House of Bath, House of Health, Tradex Catalogue and a finance company offering me a golden opportunity to put all my current debts together on one card and not pay a penny in interest for six months. That's very kind of you but I don't have any debts these days – I don't owe a brass farthing to anyone, so there.

An invitation to join the National Trust, an opportunity to win a free holiday home in Florida, and hang on, what's this? Haven't seen one of these for ages. It looks like a letter, with a first class stamp and everything: a proper letter and it's addressed to me.

I couldn't wait to open it and then I wished I hadn't. Another invitation to yet another funeral. Another old friend gone for ever. Saw him only last month – at the funeral of another old friend. We got on like a house on fire. We worked out that it must have been at least twenty-three years since we last laid eyes on one another. We said we mustn't leave it that long again – and we certainly won't. I shall be paying my last respects to him next week in a chapel somewhere in Ashby-de-la-Zouch.

I needed a break and a drop of fresh air and so I walked down the path and reversed the car out of the garage. If one isn't careful one can overdo this fresh air business.

I still had this recent spate of funerals on my mind and I couldn't help thinking that without exception the arrangements had always been spot on and the catering right on the button. No hitches, no awkward moments whatsoever.

So what about my own funeral? Should I leave it up to Aileen and the kids or should I leave a few pointers about this and that? Shame to waste all this newly acquired experience.

Perhaps we could try something different. Maybe I could lie in state for a day or so. Not for too long – don't want to overdo it. Perhaps in the library. Or better still on a table by the checkout in Sainsbury's. That would be a great idea. There would be hundreds of people filing past the coffin every hour. Especially on a Friday teatime, it's really busy then.

I became quite excited about the entire project and then quickly came down to earth with a bump when it dawned on me that I shall personally miss out on the occasion by just a few days.

I parked the car on the top of Sainsbury's roof. Not the new Sainsbury's on the ring road; the original store in the town centre that they were going to shut down once they had opened the new superstore and then didn't because it was still doing rather well.

I waited for the lift along with two teenage girls who were chatting away happily and a rather elderly couple who were trying to work out what day next week it was that their son Vernon and his wife what's-her-name were coming up to see them all the way from Aberystwyth. She had an idea they had agreed on the Thursday. She checked it out with her husband.

'What date is it today?'

'I've no idea.'

'You never know what date it is.'

'At my age you don't need to know – I'm not going anywhere.'

By the time the lift arrived we had been joined by another couple along with a tall and ruggedly good-looking young man. The two girls rather self-consciously went very quiet when he arrived, their eyes closely examining their shoes. I wanted to tell them to keep talking – they looked far prettier when their faces were alive and they were animatedly chatting away to one another.

We all waited patiently as the lift cleared and then the lot of us piled in and the doors shut behind us. As usual you could have cut the painful silence with a knife.

Then a wonderful surprise. Vernon's mother suddenly took centre stage.

'Did you know that this is a magic lift?'

Her husband closed his eyes and tried to pretend that it wasn't happening again.

'And would you like to know why, children?'

The young man and I piped up together.

'Yes-we-would.'

'Well, as we go down this lift spins round and round and round – it's a very special lift.' She spun round and round and round to illustrate her point. 'And would you like me to prove it to you, children?'

The two girls joined in with us this time and the four of us chanted together, 'Yes-we-would.'

'Well. When we got in the lift we all came in through that wall over there, didn't we?' She pointed dramatically at the wall behind us.

'Yes-we-did.'

'And now...' She half turned and swept her

176

arm out in a dramatic gesture to indicate the blank wall behind her, '...we are all going to go out through – this wall over here.'

Her timing was immaculate. Right on cue the doors behind her slid open to reveal the outside world in all its glory together with four or five people waiting with their laden trolleys and carrier bags. They stood in amazement as we gave Vernon's mother a generous round of applause and then we made our way out into the sunlight.

The two girls had come alive again and with the young man drifted off down towards the town centre, the three of them smiling and laughing together.

Come on. Let's hear it for Vernon's mother.

I decided to leave the Sainsbury's cat litter until I was on my way back and popped down to Marks & Spencer to get my weekly fix. I am addicted to their unsliced seeded batch loaves and as I entered the shop and headed for the bread section my pulse quickened and my stride lengthened. I once left it until after lunch and they had already sold out. So now I buy nine loaves at once, one for each day of the week and a couple over just in case.

The staff tend to move them about from shelf to shelf and for an awful moment my heart skipped a beat when I saw that a miserable bunch of white baps had muscled in on the seeded batch territory, but then I spotted them butted up by the pikelets on the other side of the aisles and gave them all a big squeeze before piling them into my trolley.

I had a look at my list and made my way down to Beattie's to pick up half a dozen wine glasses. They do a rather nice line in good-looking, 24 per cent lead crystal hand-cut Polish wine goblets for a very reasonable £2.99 each. Not to be sniffed at when you live with a blind woman who waves her arms about a lot.

First I popped upstairs for a quick cup of coffee and a cigarette and yet another all-in wrestling match with yet another blessed coffee machine.

I could have stood in a short queue and had my coffee made to measure for me, but I am determined to get the better of these fiendish contraptions. As I travel all over the country I come across them everywhere, often in the middle of the night, and every damned one of them is just that little bit different from the rest.

I studied the instructions, which really didn't help all that much. I don't do instructions. I get bored halfway through reading them and my mind wanders and I lose the plot, so I stood back and let an old lady go first.

She had obviously done this many times before. I watched her place her little mug beneath the left hand chrome pipe, then reach across and press the middle one of three buttons, and in no time at all she was waltzing off towards the till with a steaming mug of hot coffee. This was my kind of machine.

A little kid tried to muscle in next but I glared at him and he backed off. I stuck one of the larger mugs under the left hand chrome pipe, pressed the middle button, and, hey presto, in no time at all I also was waltzing off towards the till with a steaming mug – of foaming hot chocolate.

Quite how the old lady managed to produce hot coffee and I finished up with hot chocolate out of the same little chrome pipe I shall probably never know. I am not a great fan of hot chocolate, especially around lunchtime, but I wasn't going to let the kid know that I had screwed it up and so I decided to cut my losses.

I searched high and low for an ashtray and it wasn't until I had practically turned the place upside down that I suddenly remembered that I had given up smoking all of seven weeks, three days and some fourteen and half hours ago – but then, who's counting?

For the first time in my life I went and sat with that lot over there as opposed to sitting with us lot over here complete with the ashtrays and the crushed fag packets. It felt very strange, as though I had somehow betrayed my own brothers and sisters, and then I thought of the goldfish bowl at home into which Aileen and I had managed to stuff seven hundred pounds between us over the past seven weeks and drank a toast in hot chocolate to the wonderful John Welsby who had hypnotized the pair of us into giving it up after we had been puffing away merrily for a combined total of well over a hundred years.

I picked up my goblets and made my way into the town centre where I collected some dry cleaning from Johnson's. Not long ago I bought a casual sweater which had a suede motif on the front. It was in the sales and seemed like a bargain at the time, but that was before I came across the dreaded 'dry clean only' label. Since that fateful day Johnson's seem to have had it in their safe-keeping more often than I have had it in mine.

I love it, but it's costing me a fortune. Without even appearing to try it attracts an incredible variety of stains. I have no idea where they come from. I think jealous people throw things at me when I'm not looking.

Walking back along John William Street I turned up past the HSBC into Cloth Hall Street and remembered a most wonderful moment that happened on this very corner just a couple of weeks ago.

I had been ambling along behind a rather elderly woman who was desperately holding on to the hand of a little boy. I imagine she must have been his grandmother and I felt sorry for her. She wasn't having an easy time of it. He was playing up all the while and she was too old to be bothered with stuff like that. He wouldn't do this and he wouldn't do that. What he would do was try to swing on the end of her arm all the time until he almost had her over.

To the untrained eye he seemed to be somewhat hyperactive. To a trained eye like mine it was clear that he was being a perfect little sod.

As we crossed the road and passed in front of Carl Stuart's window a formidable-looking woman coming down the other way stopped the pair of them dead in their tracks. She spread her considerable girth across the pavement and nodded, indicating the unruly little lad.

'I see you've still got him.'

The grandmother manhandled the kid into a rather effective headlock. 'Yes. But not for much longer. Our Julie's starting work again on Monday.'

The other woman wasn't at all impressed. 'Well, you'll have him all the time then.'

But the grandmother wasn't having that. 'Oh no I won't. Our Julie's having him of a weekend. I'm having him on the Monday and the rest of the week he's going into a quiche.'

Serves the little devil right.

Aileen was up in her study when I arrived home. She was lost in a world of her own and I thought it best to leave her there whilst I put a light lunch together.

I had watched Rick Stein on the television the night before and I thought I would try one of his risottos. I love cooking programmes and make copious notes. The trouble is that when it comes down to it I rarely have all the ingredients to hand and so I mix and match and have to leave bits and pieces out altogether.

At least I had the arborio rice. I'd had it for ages and ages and I had a look all over the pack for a sell-by date, but I don't think they had got round to bothering with such new-fangled ideas in the days when I bought this packet.

I melted my butter and cooked my onions and added my stock. Rick had boiled shin beef for stock – I used a couple of Oxo cubes. He had used grated Parmesan cheese – I had to make do with Red Leicester. He handpicked fresh mushrooms from the New Forest – I found one that had done something rather disgusting in the bottom of the fridge and decided to use courgettes instead.

Despite all this it did taste like something approaching a risotto, although not necessarily from the right direction. Rick Stein would have had nothing to do with it at all, but then he's always been a bit picky.

I decided to risk it. I could have binned it and grilled Aileen a little bacon and cheese – I've got that off to a fine art – but I thought I would take a chance and popped upstairs to bring her down.

She had done whatever it was she had to do with the computer and decided that was that for a while.

'Go to sleep.'

The computer slammed shut its little door and set about doing whatever it is that computers do when they have a few moments to themselves, while I escorted my wife down to the kitchen for lunch.

'It's a risotto.'

'Right.'

Now there are many ways of saying that word. It can mean 'Fantastic'. It can mean 'Oh my God'. But when Aileen says

'Right'

it means,

'We'll wait and see, shall we?'

I sat her down and served up my dish of

the day and to my surprise it didn't look at all bad. It didn't exactly leap off the plate and say eat me, but then if it had Aileen wouldn't have noticed. The courgettes could have done with browning a little longer, but what the hell.

It's unnerving sitting down opposite her, watching her face, as she takes that first forkful, so I went and stood over by the toaster and pretended to be busy.

She took a second forkful, which is always encouraging, and then a third and a fourth, and by that time I felt relaxed enough to sit down and join her at the table.

She ate the lot and I was absolutely chuffed, even though I wasn't so keen on it myself. She scraped around the plate to see if any morsels had escaped and then sadly laid down her fork and gave me her verdict.

'That was very pleasant...'

My heart turned a perfect somersault and I decided I would go out first thing in the morning and buy Rick Stein's latest book.

'...but I don't think we'll bother again, shall we?'

We knocked back a couple of cups of coffee and had almost completed the crossword – fifteen down and twelve across were both playing hard to get – when Thermal left his radiator for what must have been the first time since the old king died, brushed up

184

against my leg, and then staggered off down to the cellar for a pee.

He didn't stay down there for long and he paused to smack his bum up against my ankle as he made his way back to base.

'That cat litter could do with a change.'

'Sorry – I forgot.'

I'll say this for Thermal, he doesn't hold a grudge. He realizes that I am only human and he makes allowances for the fact. He doubled back and very kindly let me hand-feed him several prawns from the fridge before dismissing me abruptly and staggering off towards his sheepskin rug for his early afternoon nap. He's firm, but he's fair.

I didn't want to get the car out again and so I thought I would walk up through Marsh and see if they stocked a pint-sized pack of cat litter at the Co-op. I could mix that with whatever I had left of the cats' normal stuff and they would never know the difference between that and Sainsbury's. I must live in a dream world.

I crossed the main road just above the Shell garage and took a mini detour down Mitre Street. For some reason this modest, well kept little street boasts some of the most handsome cats in Huddersfield. Sometimes they are nowhere to be seen. At other times they sprawl all over the walls, hold pyjama parties on the pavement and treat the road as though it were one huge zebra crossing.

Some wear bright collars and bells; others eschew such showy displays of bling, but if the state of their torn and tattered ears are anything to go by they are probably copiously tattooed underneath their fur, most likely with 'love' and 'hate' stamped on either paw.

If I am very lucky I sometimes catch an elderly lady as she sets off to do her weekly shop 'up Marsh'. She always has her little dog with her. He strolls along by her side, never straining at his lead, completely at peace with himself and his world, walking shoulder to shoulder along the pavement with the lady's rather independent black cat who would rather be found dead in the gutter than be seen out on a lead.

The three of them walk in step together the length of Mitre Street and then, as the main road cuts across their path and the heavy traffic intrudes into their peaceful life, the cat wishes them both well, jumps up onto a corner garden wall and sits there, never once taking her eyes off the other pair until they have disappeared up the hill and out of sight.

The little cat was making her way back down the street now and so it seemed that I had missed today's performance. I really must remember to book in advance in future.

As I passed by Don't Forget I remembered that it was our wedding anniversary at the weekend. Every year I buy a card for Aileen, preferably one with a sticky-out pattern on the front so that she can feel the picture. Then when the day arrives I place it by her coffee cup at breakfast and eventually she comes across it as she reaches out for a drink.

'What's this?'

'Your anniversary card.'

'Oh. You shouldn't have.' She opens the envelope, feels the card and then passes it over to me. 'It's lovely – what does it say?'

I read out the message to her in my best BBC voice.

'Oh, that's really lovely. Just a minute.'

She nips up to her office and brings back the same card that she has been giving me now, over and over again, for goodness knows how many years. It makes perfect sense. If she bought a fresh one each year someone else would have to pick it out for her and this way it is all her own work.

'Happy anniversary.'

'Thank you, love.'

Both cards go on the mantelpiece for a week or so and then Aileen's card mysteriously disappears back into its bright red envelope until next year.

Beverley was on duty in the shop. Alison and Paul recently bought a remote farmhouse in Spain and they were over there now, tending to the vines and digging drainage pits and sorting the thousand and one other jobs that need doing when you're daft enough to go and buy a remote farmhouse in Spain.

Beverley called me over to the counter. 'There's a message for you in the book.'

Alison had left a date-a-day diary with day-by-day instructions for the staff. Today's message for Beverley was short and sweet: 'Post the VAT envelope or you're fired.'

At the foot of the page was this short note for me: 'Tell Deric it's time for his B12 injection.'

She was dead right. I had forgotten. The months just fly by. It's good to know someone is keeping an eye on me, even when they are busy digging drains over in Spain.

I poked around the anniversary cards for a while and then the phone rang. It was Beverley's son Martin – he's a professional soldier and he's been around a bit.

'Mum. I just rang to tell you that I'm being posted out to Iraq first thing on Monday morning.'

Beverley's face went a deathly white. 'Oh no you're not.'

'Mum!'

She put her foot down. 'No. I'm sorry. You're not.'

I could just imagine Martin reporting back to his commanding officer.

'I'm sorry sir, but my mum says I can't go.'

What should have been a round trip of no more than half an hour eventually turned into a two-hour marathon. It's always the same. There is so much going on, in and around my head. So much to see, to listen to. Most of it is of little or no importance and sadly enough that's the only sort of stuff that sticks. Anything that might be useful or informative immediately self-destructs on entry.

It does have its compensations. On the way home I followed a young man through the park. He had an iPod or an ASBO or whatever it is that they are called plugged directly into his head and he made a chung-chung-chunging sound as he walked.

A couple of feet above that buzzing head of his our resident squirrel was performing a selection of his favourite dance numbers from *West Side Story* and *Oklahoma*, but the young man never noticed a thing. Head nodding, eyes down on the concrete path, he completely missed the big finish where the squirrel makes his heart-stopping, death-defying leap over to the next tree but one, the tree that always looks as though it's dying but isn't.

I was just thinking how hard it is to put into words the amount of pleasure that little squirrel had given me when I realized that I had put nothing into words all day.

Up at well before seven this morning and still not a single word engraved on the waiting computer screen, and now it was almost time for me to start preparing the evening meal.

I try. God knows I try – but life keeps getting in the way.

CHAPTER THIRTEEN

There are times, however, when it would take the hardest of hearts to begrudge me a couple of days off. Writing can be a very lonely business and you need to join up with the real world every now and then. *Lost For Words* had already provided Aileen and myself with a long weekend down in London to collect the Mental Health Award.

We missed out on a trip to Germany where we won a special commendation in the Prix Europa, but then there was New York and the Emmys and before that it was over to France to pick up the best TV film award at the Reims television festival.

I would have been off like a shot to the States once more when we won a prestigious Peabody Award, but our executive producer Keith Richardson didn't tell me about that one until he had quietly nipped over there, picked it up himself and landed safely back in Leeds.

Today Aileen and I were both curled up in the rear of a black cab heading across London towards the Dorchester and this year's BAFTA awards, and if all this sounds just a trifle pretentious and more than a little sick-making at least you have to admit that I do carry it off rather well.

The taxi tucked itself up outside the hotel and I paid the driver, over-tipping him outrageously as people who haven't been brought up to this sort of thing are often wont to do.

The next problem was to manoeuvre both Aileen and a rather large suitcase safely through the revolving door without jamming one or other of them in the mechanism. I very rarely manage to achieve this and over the years I have found that if I do have to get one of them trapped in the works then it's far less trouble in the long run if it happens to be the suitcase.

It all went rather smoothly on this occasion and after completing a mere two and half circuits I had the timing of the contraption down to a fine art and was able to hurl both of my charges out into the reception area at one and the same time.

We waited for a while as an old Arab in flowing white robes booked himself and roughly half the female population of a small desert kingdom into a rather complicated assortment of adjoining rooms and then it was my turn.

'I have a room booked in the name of Longden.'

The receptionist worked her way through

two or three pages. 'I'm sorry, sir, but I don't have anyone of that name on my list.'

A small but rather ominous black cloud appeared and hovered above my head and for one brief moment I thought I heard a muffled chuckle as it attempted to pull itself together.

'Maybe it's been booked in the name of Yorkshire Television.'

She checked. 'No – I'm afraid not.'

'Granada Television? They've sort of merged recently.'

She shook her head. 'Sorry, sir.'

Then I remembered a confirmation note that I'd tucked away in my wallet a week or so ago.

'There you are – that's the booking.'

She studied it carefully. 'You do have a room reserved.'

'Oh, good.'

'At the Grosvenor House Hotel. This is the Dorchester.'

'Right.'

'I should go over there if I were you.'

'Thank you very much. I'll do that.'

'It's only a short walk.'

We left as gracefully as we could, followed out through the door by both the sound of suppressed laughter from all those who had been waiting in the foyer and the small black cloud, who hadn't quite finished with us yet.

He controlled himself for a while and allowed us to walk perhaps fifty yards or so along Park Lane before splitting his sides and soaking us to the skin. At least I managed to throw my jacket over Aileen's new hairdo.

'I'm so sorry, love.' I don't know why she puts up with me. She could have done so much better and yet she rarely complains. I put my arm round her. 'I always seem to make a mess of things, don't I?'

'No. Not always.'

'All right – I nearly always make a mess of things.'

'I think *mostly* is the word you're looking for.'

We both started laughing and by the time we reached the Grosvenor House Hotel the laughter had taken on a hysterical edge and we just couldn't stop. We were both wet through, and the rain had started soaking up Aileen's trouser legs and had made it halfway to her knees. My shirt was hanging off me like a wet rag, the suitcase had done its level best to trigger a hernia and still we couldn't stop laughing.

We sat on a cold leather settee and tried to compose ourselves, but every now and then one of us would catch the other's eye and off we would go again.

'Why do you put up with me?'

Aileen thought about that for a moment or so.

'Well – I don't think I could ever find anyone else who would love me as much as you do.'

She has a way with words and those were such true and wonderful words that they had me blinking away the tears. Much more so than the time she told me she had already planned the inscription she would have engraved upon my headstone.

'He Meant Well.'

They did have a room waiting for us at the Grosvenor; several, in fact. The television companies had done us proud. A uniformed flunkey escorted us up and through the hotel before unlocking what I thought at first was going to be our bedroom door, until we stepped into the centre of a long private hallway that ran right to left.

We were ushered through another door at the right-hand end of the corridor and into an enormous lounge complete with a sofa, several easy chairs, a dining table for eight, an enormous television and a grand piano. I nodded in what I hoped might be taken for an intelligent manner as he pointed out this and that, and generally tried to give him the impression that we would have expected nothing less.

We had a huge bedroom at the far end of the corridor, a slightly smaller one halfway down, an absolutely fantastic marble bathroom set between the two and a well-equipped utility room where one or other of our personal maids could see to the ironing.

As soon as we were on our own Aileen sat down at the piano and proceeded to give her world famous rendition of the works of Frederic Chopin as played by the late lamented Les Dawson.

No – that's not at all fair. Aileen doesn't play the piano. She doesn't read music, has never had a lesson. But as soon as she sits down and tickles the ivories, beautiful melodies fill the air. Nothing at all in the way of a recognizable tune, but at the same time she is totally incapable of playing a bum note and the result is a wonderfully unstructured experience.

I went walkabout, unable to believe the generosity of it all. Writers don't usually come in for this sort of treatment: it's the province of those headline-grabbing actors.

I had a practice lie down on the beds and then worked my way through every wardrobe, cupboard and drawer. In the bathroom I had a practice sit on the lavatory, unwrapped the free bar of soap and tried on a shower cap before reporting back to Aileen.

She was just coming up to her grand finale. She always finishes off her performances with aplomb. This was one of those impressive endings that would have had the audience sitting in a spellbound silence for a good ten seconds before they burst into rapturous applause.

I waited for a good ten seconds then burst into rapturous applause. She bowed her head modestly.

'What about a cup of tea?'

Her slightest wish is my command and I was up and on my way before it dawned on me that the one thing I hadn't come across during my recent tour of these premises was an electric kettle.

Five luxurious rooms and no sign of a kettle. Maybe the sort of person who normally frequents this level of accommodation wouldn't even dream of juggling with a cup of hot water and a tea bag. As always Aileen had the answer.

'Ring room service.'

I hate ringing room service. I'm no good at being looked after. I always start off with an apology in case I am putting them to any sort of trouble and by the end of the call I am almost offering to come down to the kitchen and fetch it myself.

'Room service – how can I help you?'

I apologized for troubling him, ordered tea for two and left it at that. Maybe I'm growing up.

It was a good half hour before it arrived and when I opened the door I could see why. The man with the tray was what one might describe as an old retainer. He had probably been in the service of the hotel throughout both world wars and quite possibly the great fire of London.

I saw him off with one of my ridiculous tips, which meant he could now put at least two of his great-grandchildren through university, then poured out the tea, which by this time was well past its best and best left alone.

That night, resplendent in our evening glad rags, we made our way downstairs to the Grosvenor's enormous ballroom and the British Academy of Film and Television Arts awards ceremony. The hotel was absolutely bursting at the seams with faces that would have normally entered my world only via the small screen at home.

Aileen becomes quite disoriented in a crowd like this. The world closes in on her; voices merge with each other until they become a single jarring noise that surrounds her, hems her in and makes her feel quite nauseous.

So I talk to her all the time, letting her know where we are, what this is, what that was, who said this, who said that and whether the person who spoke to her over there was a he or a she, and I must admit that there would be times during the evening when it was going to be difficult to be absolutely sure.

I remembered the day we first met. It was at a literary lunch. We had been placed next to each other at the dinner table and she turned to me with a grimace as she adjusted something or other under cover of the table-cloth.

'Don't these blessed teddies pull you up around the crutch?'

'I've no idea, love – I don't wear them myself.'

Her eyes widened in surprise at the sound of my voice.

'I'm so sorry – I didn't realize you were a man.'

It's not the sort of remark that fills a chap with confidence, especially since I had no idea at the time that she couldn't see me.

As we slowly manoeuvred our way through the crowd towards the head of a huge winding staircase I continued to try to keep Aileen aware of what was going on in the mass of humanity that swirled around her, but I am not very good at putting names to faces.

Aileen heard a familiar voice as it pulled up alongside her and gestured for me to listen by waving with her right hand, in-advertently stroking the left breast of the rather gorgeous woman who happened to be brushing past.

'I'm terribly sorry.'

The woman smiled as she moved away. 'That's all right. I quite enjoyed it.'

Aileen laughed and then turned to me. 'I know that voice – who was it?'

'Joanna Lumley.'

'Of course.'

I'm no good at remembering faces, but bodies like Joanna Lumley's are a completely different matter altogether.

We reached the top of the staircase and had only negotiated our way down the first couple of steps when we came up behind a huge shape that seemed to cut out most of the light.

Through the murk I could make out the expensively suited back of Lennox Lewis, who had recently become the heavyweight boxing champion of the world after beating the living daylights out of Mike Tyson. He was standing two or three steps below us but still he towered well above my head.

There were five of us crowded shoulder to shoulder on our step, but he had a step all to himself and he needed it. He was enormous – it was as though someone had plonked a double wardrobe down right in front of us.

His height was impressive enough, but I couldn't get over the width of his back and shoulders. How could anyone be daft enough to get in the ring with a man that size? I'd rather be thrown to the lions any time.

Aileen was on my left arm, where she had the extra security of the banister rail, and to my right was an actor whose name had been tossed about at length during an early casting meeting for *Lost For Words*. I was all for him at the time; he seemed to fit the bill perfectly. Now, as we slowly manoeuvred our way down the staircase, I was able to listen to him off duty, working without a script.

Other Man: 'So I told him he could stick it up his backside.'

Our Actor: 'I don't know. What are you like?'

Other Man: 'Well, if you give 'em a yard they'll take a mile.'

Our Actor: 'Tell me about it.'

Other Man: 'And it's not as if it's the first time.'

Our Actor: 'Tell me about it.'

Other Man: 'I just don't let him get away with anything any more.'

Our Actor: 'I don't know. What are you like?'

Other Man: 'It's the only way.'

Our Actor: 'Tell me about it.'

I'm not a religious man, but I felt that I should cross myself immediately and thank the Lord for delivering unto us the wonderful Pete Postlethwaite.

Eventually we made it down to our table in

the main hall and joined the other members of our company. Sita Jackson our producer, Keith Richardson the executive producer, Dame Thora and her daughter Janette Scott-Rademaekers, together with Pete Postlethwaite and his delightful wife Jacqui.

Lost For Words had been nominated for Best Single Drama, Thora was up for Best Actress and Pete for Best Actor and so each of us had a chance of picking up a Bafta, but we had been pitted against some pretty stiff competition.

In the meantime we settled down to enjoy the food, the company and the occasion, and as we worked our way through the meal I became more and more thankful that I was one of those lucky faces behind the screen rather than one that had long ago imprinted itself on everyone's memory.

Pete and Thora hardly had time to put a fork to their mouths as hordes of people came over to have 'a quick word' with them. Sometimes they were old friends who were more than welcome, but more often than not they were total strangers intent on working the room.

At last the awards ceremony got under way and we watched as four roving television cameras slipped around the room, swooping in and out, one on each of the four nominees in every category. They would then record for posterity the undiluted ecstasy of the winner and the muffled agony of the three losers, all of whom had to try to look as though they thoroughly approved of the judges' decision and smile broadly as they generously clapped the winner all the way up to the rostrum. At a nearby table the cast of *Coronation Street* gave us an object lesson in how to go about this by standing and clapping the winning *EastEnders* team as they danced their way up onto the stage whilst muttering through their wide and generous smiles, 'Bugger – bugger – bugger.'

Then in no time at all it was our turn to have a camera parked by the side of the table as the four nominations for Best Single Drama were shown on four separate screens.

The tension mounted until the inevitable envelope was produced and then came the announcement.

'And the winner is...'

We produced the necessary smiles and kept them going on full beam throughout a dramatic pause that seemed to go on for ever.

'And the winner is... *The Murder of Stephen Lawrence.*'

'Bugger – bugger – bugger.'

The evening fell a little flat for a while after that, but then brightened considerably as we approached the award for Best Actor. I looked over to my right to wish Pete the best of luck but he wasn't there. I turned to Jacqui who was sitting next to his vacant chair.

'Where is he?'

'On the toilet.'

'But it's any minute now.'

She shrugged. 'He knows that – he's a law unto himself.'

I had to do something and so I hared off to the nearest gents and walked down the line of cubicles.

'Pete – are you in there?'

I received a variety of replies including an invitation from someone who asked if I would care to join him. I made my excuses and moved on. Eventually I struck gold and through the closed door came the dulcet tones of our leading man.

'What?'

'You're due on any second now.'

'Don't worry – I shan't win.'

'You might.'

'No chance – be Michael Gambon again, he's on a roll.'

'What if you're wrong?'

'You go and pick it up for me.'

I made it back to the table just in time, all the while rehearsing an acceptance speech in my head.

'I'm afraid Pete Postlethwaite can't be with us tonight – he happens to be on the toilet at the moment.'

The four cameras – the four clips up there on the big screen – the dreaded envelope.

'And the winner is ... *Michael Gambon.*'

I smiled generously through gritted teeth for the second time that evening.

'Bugger – bugger – bugger.'

Two down with only one more to go, and Thora was up against some very strong competition for the Best Actress award in the shape of Maggie Smith, Francesca Annis and Lindsay Duncan. On top of that she had won this very award only twelve months ago. Would the judges want her to win it twice in consecutive years?

We would soon find out. The only person at the table who wasn't the slightest bit nervous seemed to be the great Dame herself, but then she always was a very good actress.

The cameraman breathed a sigh of relief as he organized his close-up of Thora. He'd had a panic attack a little while ago when he had zoomed in on Pete only to find that he was filming an empty chair.

The big moment arrived.

'And the winner is...'

We held our collective breath.

'Dame Thora Hird.'

The applause that exploded from all round the room almost took the roof off and was so genuine that it was still as warm as toast as Sita Jackson and myself slowly eased our leading lady painfully up the long, long ramp and onto the stage.

It took us some time. Thora could have used the wheelchair or even been presented with her award at the table – but no, this would probably be the last time she was ever going to do this and she was going to do it properly.

It would be her eighty-ninth birthday in a week's time and she couldn't have wished for a better present.

With no cats to hassle us I didn't exactly leap out of bed the next morning. I took my time and after a while I sort of dribbled out, bit by bit, until I was kneeling on the bed-side rug. Aileen sat up and gave a great big stretch, still tucked under the enormous white sheet, and for a moment it looked as though I had spent the night with a fully paid up member of the Ku Klux Klan.

'I could murder a cup of tea.'

Me too. I had a word with my reluctant limbs and eventually managed to persuade them that it would be to everyone's benefit if we all pulled together as a team. After a lot of moaning and groaning we managed to make it across the bedroom floor and out into the corridor, but in no time at all we were back by the bedside.

'We haven't got a kettle.'

I couldn't face dealing with room service again and so we dressed in silence and then crept down for breakfast and sat there like a couple of zombies until a large pot of tea, bacon and eggs twice and a huge pot of coffee gradually began to turn us back into the two warm and wonderful human beings that we undoubtedly are.

We had a chat with *The Royle Family's* Ricky Tomlinson whom we'd met last night as he arrived for the BAFTAs with his wife tucked under one arm and a twelve-pack of best bitter tucked under the other.

'I couldn't be sure they'd have any down here.'

Before I fastened the suitcase I went through the apartment once again, room by room, drawer by drawer, looking for any of our bits and pieces that I might have overlooked and making a mental note to pack a travelling kettle the next time we went away.

It was just as well I checked. In the bath-room I found a Grosvenor shower cap, a virgin bar of soap, a bottle of shampoo and another of conditioner that Aileen had missed the first time round. You can never be too careful.

As I manoeuvred both wife and suitcase out of the bedroom and down the hallway Aileen caught her elbow against the handle of a door I hadn't noticed before. It was set back at a slight angle and was probably a blanket store.

'What was that?'

'I think it's a cupboard.'

I turned the handle and there laid out before me was a fully fitted kitchen complete with a fridge and a freezer, a microwave and a proper oven, a dishwasher, a toaster and yard after yard of working space surrounding a double draining sink unit, by the side of which stood a large chrome kettle.

'Bugger – bugger – bugger.'

'I take back yesterday's mostly,' said Aileen. 'You were right the first time when you said always.'

CHAPTER FOURTEEN

I spent the next morning clearing up a backlog of letters and bills. I'm not very good at working my way through a pile of letters. I start off as though I am shaping a new book, waste far too much time writing and rewriting, trying to get my first effort absolutely spot on, and then don't have time enough to make a proper job of the others.

I jacked it in at lunchtime, took a glass of wine and went and sat on the garden wall with Thermal as he looked out over the park. Happy childish laughter came tumbling past us as a slightly built Muslim woman shepherded her two bubbling young boys along the pavement below, then steered them carefully across the road, only releasing her charges once the three of them had planted their feet down on the green green grass of Greenhead Park.

The lads were around five years old and one of them had three cricket stumps tucked underneath his arm, the other a single stump and a bat. Once they had been set free they charged off to sort out a likely pitch for themselves and then began pacing it out and hammering in the stumps.

Their mother followed on in a gentle, ladylike stroll, never once taking her eyes off her two budding sportsmen. Her eyes were all that she deigned to show to the world as, swathed in a voluminous black robe complete with hijab, she kept tabs on her young family through a small open slit half the size of a letter box.

One of the boys took guard with the bat and the other assumed the responsibilities of the wicket-keeper, both of them crouching low as they awaited the emergence of a non-existent bowler.

And then, as the nun-like mother closed in on the two waxwork figures, she produced something from somewhere deep inside her robe, and from about ten metres she suddenly burst into a vigorous sprint. With an action that would have had Glenn McGrath open-mouthed in admiration, she hurled down the first ball of her opening over.

It was a bouncer, just an inch or so short of a length, and it flew past the batsman's eyebrows and raced to the boundary for four byes. Her follow-through took her within a few intimidating feet of the batsman. She gave him a couple of pointers, adjusted his stance and then strode back to her mark.

She got him with her fifth ball, his stumps flying in all directions, and Thermal and I applauded loudly. Her action was remarkable, a violent mixture of flailing arms, legs and rippling midnight cloth, under which flashed a pair of startlingly white trainers.

She disposed of the second batsman in no time at all and then took her turn at the wicket. The lads tried their best but she soon had them racing all over the park as she hooked and pulled and drove them to distraction.

Tigger had joined us by this time and the three of us sat enthralled by the scene that was being played out in front of us.

I first came across the two boys some weeks ago when their father brought them down to the park. He and his wife came over from Iran a few years ago but he had developed nothing like the natural talent that she had just displayed. His English was somewhat fractured to say the least and the two little boys had translated for him in broad Yorkshire accents.

Now they were providing the same service for their mother. An elderly and somewhat genteel lady dressed in expensive-looking paisley had strayed onto the pitch and stopped for a chat, holding up play. The lads quickly sorted it out and soon had her acting as wicket-keeper, with her two Marks & Spencer's carrier bags fielding at first and second slip.

I could have sat there all day but I had a wife to feed and the two cats were beginning to drop hints.

'*Throw something at him, Tigger. He's in a world of his own.*'

There came the sound of footsteps down the garden path and Aileen appeared round the corner of the house. She stared hard at a tall thin bush in the far corner.

'Is that you?'

The bush seemed to be somewhat pre-occupied and had no idea she was talking to him, so I took over the responsibility.

'Near enough, love. Are you ready for lunch?'

Right on cue her stomach rumbled noisily like a tumble dryer on heat. She seemed to consider that to have stated her case perfectly well, and turned on her heels. The three of us rose to our collective ten feet and followed her into the house.

I fed the four of us and then went out into the courtyard to check up on Nokia. He hadn't looked at all well earlier on and it seemed to me that he had taken a turn for the worse.

He was hidden away in his basket under the back steps but I could hear him wheezing from halfway across the yard. I called his name and he came out of his little hideaway to have a word with me. He looked an absolute mess. His eyes and nose were all bunged up and his body language had a very sad story of its own to tell.

Back in the kitchen I told Aileen. 'I think he's got cat flu and I don't quite know what to do with him.'

If he had been anything like a normal pet I could have bundled him into the cat carrier and whisked him off to the vet, but what we had prowling around in our back yard was the nearest thing to the Beast of Bodmin Moor that you were ever likely to find in West Yorkshire.

'It's just impossible to touch him.'

'Ring the AA.'

'Do what?'

'Sorry - the RSPCA.'

So I did, and by mid-afternoon they were already on the case, represented by the rather attractive Inspector Swift.

She listened to what I had to say and had the good sense to keep a couple of feet between herself and Nokia as she weighed him up.

'There's no doubt about it – it's definitely cat flu, but I'm afraid it's your problem and not ours.'

'How do you mean?'

'Well, we only deal with injured animals, ferals and homeless strays and he's your cat.'

'No, he's not my cat. He just happens to live in my garden.'

At that moment Nokia jumped up on the sleeper, his tail brushing my legs as he took a deep drink from the fountain. He rolled his damp eyes and looked at me adoringly. Inspector Swift had all the evidence she needed.

'Well, he thinks he is.'

She left me a voucher so that I could have his testicles removed absolutely free of charge and I thought that maybe I should mention her kind offer to Nokia. He would be thrilled. She also arranged to have a special RSPCA cage delivered so that I could catch him without losing an arm or a leg or too much blood.

I knew it wasn't going to work with Nokia the moment I set eyes on it. A long steel contraption, it incorporated a rather complicated mechanism that operated a wicked-looking trap-door. It would slam shut the moment he stepped onto a metal platform in order to get at a saucer of food.

Nokia would rather starve to death than stick his head in through that ominous-looking door.

'Well, it could take several days, but once he gets hungry enough...'

I tried for the best part of an afternoon, but there was no way I could watch him starve for the rest of the day, let alone the best part of a week.

I didn't know what to do. I have always been bad at anything that involves me declaring: 'It's going to hurt, but it's for your own good.' And so I helped him to a saucer of seconds and sat down on Aileen's garden bench to have a good think, but before I could shift my mind out of neutral and into the appropriate gear our old friend the squirrel burst onto the scene.

He came scurrying along the top of the courtyard wall and then ran straight down the sheer surface of the garden gate. Closed gates present no challenge to the average squirrel. They work as a sort of vertical drawbridge, designed to make one's entrance at the same time both easier and more spectacular.✗

His relationship with the crow seems to have come to a natural end and maybe it's for the best. They were good for one another in many ways but it would never have worked out in the long run – there were too many differences. Her feathers for one, his furry tail for another. His annoying little habit of stuffing nuts in his cheeks, hers of flying off in a huff. But above all there was always going to be that age gap – it very rarely works.

He scampered across the courtyard and made straight for Nokia's bowl of nourishing Iams biscuits. They do have a nut-like quality about them and a hungry squirrel isn't about to split hairs. He greedily began to tuck them away into the expanding

215

pouches that nature has provided for him.

Nokia looked on in amazement. If I had tried to steal his biscuits he would have had me for breakfast, but he has never known quite what to make of the squirrel and shows him a nervous respect that he has never shown to me.

But then the squirrel took what proved to be a step too far. He nipped into Nokia's kennel to sort out his nuts. Now Nokia's kennel is a no-go area even for dead leaves. If an arthritic leaf, tottering on its last legs, happens to limp in through the open door crying 'Sanctuary – sanctuary', what it finishes up with is a clip round the earhole and a damn good shredding.

The squirrel didn't stand a chance. Nokia was in there like a shot and from deep within the bowels of the kennel came the amplified sounds of a momentous battle before the squirrel emerged like a bullet from a gun and ran straight in through the open door of the RSPCA's steel trap.

Nokia would have been in there after him if the squirrel hadn't panicked and jumped hard onto the metal platform, activating the spring mechanism.

The door slammed shut. Steel bars now separated the two adversaries and it seemed rather doubtful that their relationship would ever be the same again.

I joined Nokia at the cageside and together we examined our catch. You would have been proud of the little squirrel. He wasn't one to panic in public. He certainly wasn't happy about the situation in which he found himself but he was damned if he was going to show it. He reminded me of a John Mills character displaying a stiff upper lip in one of those ancient prisoner of war films and I half expected him to produce a vaulting horse from somewhere about his person.

I considered my options. I could take him to the vet's and have him castrated – I had the RSPCA voucher in the kitchen drawer and it didn't seem to rule out squirrels – or I could let him loose in the park and gain his undying gratitude.

I have always put great store by undying gratitude. Sometime in the future he could turn out to be the squirrel who never forgets and one day drag me out of the path of a runaway horse or lie with me after I have collapsed in a snowstorm, keeping me alive with the warmth of his little body. So I let him loose.

Or rather I tried to. I took him over to the park, sat the cage down on the grass, removed the steel shutter and pointed his nose out towards the wide open spaces and neatly trimmed flower beds.

He didn't want to know. He just sat there and rather delicately began to wash his face and whiskers. So I tipped the cage forward to an angle of forty-five degrees and gently slid him out on his bottom, back into his natural environment, at which point he once again became the lovable streetwise urchin that we have all come to know and steer clear of.

He sailed up the gnarled old trunk of his favourite tree, sat himself down on a handy branch and swore profusely at the world in general and at me in particular.

Back in the courtyard it looked as though the recent squirrel wars had been a step too far for poor old Nokia. He lay on the mat in the back porch looking absolutely knackered, his eyes gummed up and all but closed, his breath rattling in his chest.

I had to do something but I didn't know what. The RSPCA's cage wasn't going to be the answer, not this time. If only his kennel had a door on it that I could slam shut once he was in there.

Hang on a moment – the cat carrier down in the cellar had a door and it did look a bit like his kennel in a fading light, especially if you were the sort of cat whose eyes were all bunged up and who was as thick as two short planks.

Who knows? It just might work. I nipped down to the cellar, dusted it off and brought it up to the courtyard. Nokia was gasping his way through what was left of the pile of biscuits on his saucer and took not the slightest notice of me. He had enough on as it was. He would take a brief nibble and then have to come up and fight for air.

Without his seeing a thing I quietly tucked his kennel away in the dustbin shed and slipped the carrier into place. It worked like a charm. Eating and breathing at the same time was getting far too much for him to handle and he decided to have a bit of a lie down in the privacy of his own kennel.

I slammed the door shut behind him and he went berserk. The trick now would be to click the two latches on the grill and make it fast without shedding too much blood.

I had a go at it and I shed blood, lots of blood. Roughly an armful. The battalions of pills I am taking these days seem to have thinned the stuff down so that it pours out at the slightest provocation. Whenever I bleed I bleed for England.

But at least on this occasion I had triumphed. I had him under lock and key, and a blanket spread over the top of the contraption quietened him down somewhat whilst I left him on his own for a moment and went to work with the Savlon and a roll of Elastoplast.

A quarter of an hour later I triumphantly carried him, kicking and screaming, into Donaldson's reception area. I had never been here before but this was the veterinary practice specified on the RSPCA's voucher and I was very impressed with the set-up. It looked most professional.

There were several miserable-looking cats and a vastly outnumbered fox terrier waiting to be seen. A sad little rabbit lay tucked up in a cardboard box on the seat next to an incredibly boring parrot with far too much to say for itself, thankfully muffled somewhat by a colourful blanket which had been thrown over his cage.

Under his much plainer blanket Nokia quietened down as I carried him over to the desk.

'Hello. His name's Nokia. I think he has cat flu.'

'In that case take him straight back out to the car park. We'll come and fetch you when we're ready for him.'

I should have had more sense. Cat flu can be a killer and those poor felines lined up in reception looked as though they had more than enough to cope with as it was without catching something nasty from a fellow patient.

We must have waited in the car park for half an hour or so. Nokia was very quiet now and shaking like a leaf. I felt so sorry for him. Today's experiences must have been terrifying. He had never been in a cage before, never been in a car. He had no idea how to interact with either human beings or other cats.

Since arriving on my doorstep as a tiny kitten he had never once ventured outside the courtyard and he knew nothing of the outside world. He hadn't learned a single thing that might have come in useful to him as he eventually embarked on his present career as a cat.

My fault, I suppose. I had provided him with everything he thought he needed in life and he hadn't bothered looking for anything else. He had been with us for over a year now and I still hadn't been able to break through that solid wall of distrust.

'We're ready for him now.' An attractive young woman had appeared out of nowhere and was peeling the blanket from the cage. 'What's his name?'

'Nokia.'

'Right – let's have him inside.'

She led the way and I carried him through the reception area to an examination room in the back of the building.

Nokia had given up. He slumped on the floor of the cat carrier, defeat written all over him.

'He isn't well at all, is he? We'd better keep him in. He's going to need a series of injections.'

She made to open the carrier door but I warned her of how violent he could be and

221

she sensibly changed her mind.

'Never mind – we'll sort him out. I'm the vet who will be looking after him, by the way. My name is Kat Arnold.'

CHAPTER FIFTEEN

The day started with a very welcome telephone call. The *Countess of Evesham* had been completely rebuilt and refitted and with a bit of luck and a following wind would be ready for business once again by the weekend.

It had taken a mere six weeks but it had seemed more like six months as Nick and Lisa had battled to get the boat back to Stratford for the Christmas rush, at the same time transforming a dowdy old café cum billiard hall in Nice into a plush new restaurant of which they could be justifiably proud. Karrs was due to open in just over a month.

Nick was to stay in France and see to things over there whilst Lisa got the boat back up the Avon and brought in some much-needed cash. Not a single penny had found its way into the till during those six hectic weeks, the expenses had been enormous and there had been valued and much-loved staff to keep on the books.

It's at such times that you take a good long look at your kids and proudly say to yourself, 'I didn't do such a bad job there.'

I couldn't say the same about Nokia. I called in at the vet's later that morning to see how he was getting on. The receptionist told me that he had broken out of his cage not long after I had dropped him off. He'd had a go at all and sundry and run riot, drawing blood and causing absolute chaos throughout every room in the building until they finally managed to corner him and pin him to the floor about half an hour or so later.

'The vet will be with you in a moment. She'll tell you all about it.'

I sat myself down on a long leather bench and waited my turn to have a few moments alone with the infamous inmate.

Sitting next to me was an elderly woman who had extremely bad breath and a miserable excuse for a tortoise perched on her knee. At least I believe it was a tortoise. She certainly had a shell on her knee. Whether it contained a tortoise or not I shall never be absolutely sure. If he was in there he wasn't about to stick anything out through any of the available orifices – perhaps it was his way of dealing with the bad breath.✗

Sitting on the other side of her was the young woman who had been here yesterday with the blanketed parrot. Today his cage was uncovered and the girl was making soothing noises through the bars. He didn't look at all well and seemed to have taken the cares of the world upon his shoulders – that is if parrots have shoulders. I've never really thought about it until now. The older woman frowned at the bird in disgust.

'I can't be doing with birds meself. I'm looking after me daughter's budgie while she's away. I've had me instructions. I'm not allowed to have a bloody fag in 'same bloody room as him – I'm not allowed to light me bloody candles and she says I'm not to use me hair spray on 'pain of death. So I've gone and stuck him out in 'garage. I think it's best for both of us.'

A young girl escorted me through to the back of the building and there was poor old Nokia, lying miserably on his cage floor, staring into space, his dead eyes telling the world a dreadful story of defeat.

'He led us quite a dance.'

'So I believe.'

'He's not a very nice cat, is he?'

I wanted to defend him, to make excuses for him, but I couldn't find the words. He was as thick as a short plank. He was both vicious and a congenital coward at the same time and had no redeeming qualities whatsoever.

When I had taken him on as a young lad he had been all set to follow in his father's footsteps. To carry on the family tradition and become a flea-bitten feral, a killing machine, to think only of himself, never to trust another soul and eventually to die an extremely lonely and very painful death as do all wild animals.

Now I had taken over the responsibility for his life and he had no need to go looking for food any more – it appeared twice a day as though by magic. He had his own neat little apartment with a most comfortable bedroom and, across the courtyard, a carpeted kennel for daytime use with running water that ran almost up to his front door, together with a vast lavatory over on the rockery where he was able to bury his bright yellow deposits at will. Unfortunately the rockery hadn't been fitted with a flushing system. But not to worry, he had this little man they called Deric who reported for duty twice a day with an enormous trowel and a plastic bag. It wasn't a bad life, but still he would attempt to remove one of my fingers if I so much as tried to touch him.

And now he looked as though death would be a welcome alternative. He had never been enclosed in a room before this week, never mind a cage. Then these evil people had overpowered him, imprisoned him, stuck needles in him and removed both his testicles without so much as a by your leave.

I pressed my face close to the bars and tried to attract his attention, but his dead

eyes would have nothing to do with me.
'It's all your fault.'

When I had first walked into the room, the cage next to Nokia had appeared to be empty but as I stared at my gummy-eyed cat and wondered why I was spending all this money on something that wouldn't even give me the time of day, I heard a rustling and a plaintive cheep coming from next door. Then out of the corner of my eye I noticed something rather weird emerging from under a pile of dried grass.

I moved in closer to get a better look and the strangest little bird I have ever seen in my life emerged from its bed of straw and raced over to say hello.

Although it was still nothing but a bit of a kid it stood around some twenty centimetres tall and most of that imposing height consisted of a featherless neck that went on for ever and hovered above a thin pair of bald legs that would have looked ridiculous in tights. Stuck in between this extraordinary neck and the long knobbly legs was a miserable excuse for a body about half the size of a shuttlecock.

There was a small card Sellotaped to the foot of his cage and I bent over for a better look.

Baby Albatross.

What on earth would a baby albatross be

doing here in Huddersfield? I made a point of asking the girl the minute she came back.

'One of our clients found him walking down the middle of the main Wakefield road and brought him in.'

With that she opened the cage and sat the little bird down on her shoulder. He adjusted his legs, made himself comfortable and peered deep into her left ear.

'He likes to have a good look round every day. He's very inquisitive.'

He politely nodded goodbye and the two of them disappeared to go and have a good look round as I tried to come to terms with the idea of a baby albatross walking through Huddersfield down the middle of the busy Wakefield road.

Kat Arnold had finished for the day, but one of her colleagues came and filled me in with a report on Nokia's progress. Apparently he hadn't progressed all that far and his cat flu was still a source of deep concern.

'We'll keep him here for a couple more days and complete his course of injections. Then we'll have a better idea.'

Stuck in the five o'clock traffic on the way back home, just me and an empty cat transporter on the passenger seat, listening to the PM programme going on about the honours list and the various awards being dished out to our politicians, our sportsmen and a whole host of film and television personalities – the more I heard, the more I cherished the honour given to the coach of the Greek national football team after they had managed at long last to conquer their rivals from Portugal. He was given permission to drive his car in the bus lanes whenever he wished.

I could have done with an honour like that as I limped along in the rush hour traffic, but at least I had the time to take a good look round me at the bits and pieces of Huddersfield that I generally ignore as I race round the ring road at thirty to forty miles an hour – fifty if there is no one looking.

Sadly I had left the Wakefield road without coming across any sign of a broken-hearted albatross wandering up and down the tarmac looking for its young. I had been aching to wind down my window and shout, 'Don't worry. The vet is taking care of him and he's as happy as Larry.'

A tear of gratitude would have rolled down the face of the albatross and it would have made both our days.

I was now inching my way past the university, which has settled down wonderfully and is becoming a more venerable institution by the hour.

When it first took on the mantle of a university many a year ago it seemed like some spotty teenager starting out on the first day of a new job, all ill at ease and poncing up and down in a new suit, not quite knowing what it was supposed to be doing.

But now, all this time later, as it spreads its way along the ring road and out along the canal, taking on, refurbishing and absorbing a wonderful collection of old buildings and churches that seem to have been waiting for this moment all their lives, it could have been with us for ever.

Last year it decided in its wisdom to take Aileen and me into the fold. We were both presented with honorary degrees, which Aileen, as a native of the town and a novelist with some thirty-five books to her name, fully deserved. Her husband, this miserable little lad who failed his eleven-plus, made a hell of a mess of his O levels and left school behind him at the tender age of sixteen, was also made an Honorary Doctor of Letters and yet he still can't spell squirrel without looking it up.

It's surprising how many of the university students fall in love with Huddersfield and decide to stay on and live here after graduating. I sometimes think that we 'comers-in' are the ones who really appreciate the warmth and the depth of the town, but occasionally I think we are fighting a losing battle.

A few years ago Aileen and I were up in

Scotland, at a writers' conference in Irwin Bridge, and we sat down for a meal with two delightful ladies from Edinburgh.

'And whereabouts is it that you come from?' Mary wanted to know.

'Huddersfield in West Yorkshire.'

'Well now,' she said. 'There's a coincidence. Some time ago, when the hotels were doing those cheap weekend breaks, I spent a long weekend in Huddersfield.'

Her friend stared at her in amazement.

'What!' she cried. 'Deliberately?'

As I reached home and pulled the car into the garage I listened to a rather twee representative of the fashion industry being interviewed on Radio 4. He had been introduced as a designer of 'ready-to-wear ties' and I sat there in the car for quite a while and listened to him as I tried to work out exactly what other types of ties there might be available on the market.

I never found out. He went on and on about nothing in particular until I found myself drifting away and wondering if I had enough white emulsion paint left in the cellar to give the garage ceiling a couple of coats as well as the walls.

As Alan Bennett's father said after listening to one of his sister-in-law's interminable stories, 'I wouldn't care, but you're no further on when she's done.'

I pulled Nokia's empty cat transporter from the car and stuck it on the top of the high garden wall. It's a very handy wall. Round about six foot tall when viewed from the lane, it comes in at an even handier three feet and a bit once you have pushed open the front gate and climbed the few steps into the elevated garden.

When I've done the weekly shopping down at Sainsbury's I empty the car boot and push all the bulky stuff, the odd case of red wine, the twelve rolls of white toilet paper, the odd case of red wine I've bought just in case and the other odd case of red wine that I've bought just to be on the safe side, on top of the high garden wall. Then I have only to carry the shopping bags full of tiddly little bits and pieces down the lane, in through the front gate and up the garden path.

Having dumped them down on the kitchen table I nip out of the back door, ease the heavy stuff off the wall and ferry it the few yards into the house. It works like clockwork and saves on those dodgy knees and impending hernias when you get to my age.

However, on this occasion Aileen had beaten me to it. She was already out there bending over and chatting to the empty cat transporter on the garden wall.

'How are you feeling, my little love?'

The metal cage declined to answer.

'You'll soon be right as rain and back in your own little house.'

The cage continued to sulk.

Aileen shifted position and tried again from a slightly different angle. She daren't get too close – it was the sort of cage that could give you a nasty nip if you weren't careful.

'Never mind, love. You'll feel a lot better now you are safe at home.'

I held back and tried to work out what to do. If I charged up and told her that she had just spent the last couple of minutes talking to a completely empty cage she would be terribly embarrassed. Anyone with the smallest degree of sensitivity who had witnessed the scene would have found it a touching experience – anyone that is except Aileen, who expects far too much of herself.

I decided to pretend it hadn't happened and made the noise of someone who is in a hell of a rush and hasn't heard a thing. This involves the heavy breathing of a distracted man who has just arrived that very second from somewhere else and is about to return there on an extremely urgent mission that just can't wait.

I bent and grabbed the empty cage from the wall.

'He's still not right. The vet's decided it would be best to keep him in for another day or so.'

I raced off to deal with the job that just couldn't wait and a few moments later Aileen joined me in the kitchen. She began to sift through the carrier bags on the table.

'I thought they would,' she said. 'These things take time.'

That evening turned out to be the sort of evening that makes you wonder why you ever bother tarting yourself up to eat out.

The battle through the traffic to some fancy new restaurant that might or might not live up to the word of mouth that's been put about recently. Not being able to finish off the bottle of red wine because you have just realized that you had a glass at lunch-time and the police have let it be known that they are having a clampdown. The indigestion when the bill arrives.

So that evening the car stayed in the garage and I had a quiet meal at home with the woman I love and for once I managed to serve her a dish for which no apology was necessary.

The fish would have given its life willingly had it known it was going to look as good as this, and the asparagus turned out to be firm but fair. I love asparagus, but more often than not I overdo it and it lands on the plate all limp-wristed and feeling sorry for itself. Today it was absolutely perfect. Undeniably butch and yet not frightened to show its caring side. The accompanying salad was both exotic and inventive and yet tempered with a certain amount of restraint.

I have been introduced to a wide variety of seeds and nuts recently and I do tend to get carried away on occasions. Pine nuts, sesame and sunflower seeds accompany a veritable lorryload of pumpkin seeds, all of them scattered like gravel throughout the salad.

Recently Aileen told me that she thought I'd overdone it again.

'It rattled as you brought it to the table.'

But not on this occasion. Everything fell into place, the wine was a belter and over the coffee we completed the *Daily Telegraph* crossword in record time. I got twenty-four across all on my own and Aileen sorted out the rest in no time at all.

Then Sally rang and wanted to know how I was. Over the past year, as my health has deteriorated, the kids have been on the telephone at least every other day.

'How are you feeling, Dad?'

'Fine.'

'Oh, I am pleased. Could I just have a quick word with Aileen?'

In a soft voice to Aileen, 'How is he really?'

She brought me up to date with the latest news and told me that Katie's new friend had stayed for tea that afternoon.

'I should tell you, Mrs French, that I am a vegetarian. In fact I am a piscetarian – I only eat fish.'

Sally thought about that for a moment.

'Is it a problem, Mrs French?'

'How about fish and chips?'

'Oh, that would be wonderful.'

Some problems are there to be sorted.

Katie came on the phone and we chatted away happily for some time. She's almost fourteen now, and since I am fast approaching my second childhood from the opposite direction our conversation just rattles along these days.

I remembered the time when she was half that age and we went along to Bradford to have a look round the National Museum of Photography, Film and Television. Towards the end of our tour we came across a gold Emmy award standing to attention in a glass case.

Sally indicated the Emmy with a discreet nod and I answered her by simply raising an eyebrow. Wouldn't do to show off, would it? But Katie hadn't yet been weighed down by the formal restraints of adulthood.

'You've got one of those at home, haven't you, Grampy?'

'Yes, darling.'

Immediately all eyes were on me.

'I wonder who he is?'

'I'm sure I've seen him on the telly.'

236

'So have I – oh hell, it's on the tip of my tongue.'

Sally and I scooped up Katie and disappeared into the crowd. The limelight is the stuff of life for actors and all those self-styled celebrities. Writers are better keeping well out of it.

Still, bless the child. It was quite fun being the mysterious stranger for a change and I gave her a hug and great big kiss on the way out.

CHAPTER SIXTEEN

I must have been born lucky. Another hair-
cut – another anecdote. Trudy had just
about sorted me out. She was fiddling away
with the comb and scissors round at the
back of my head where she knows I can
never quite tell what's going on.

She never bothers to ask me how I want it,
because we both know that I'm going to get
it how she wants it and it's better left like
that because she knows what she's doing
and I don't.

A mirror appeared by my left ear, then
quickly whipped round the back of my neck
at a rate of knots and hovered for a while by
my right ear. She must have cut off all those
rather attractive grey curls that nestled in
the nape of my neck, the curls that I had
been nurturing for the past few weeks – the
curls that would make me look like a proper
writer.

'What do you think?'

'I think you've taken advantage of me
again.'

'You should be so lucky.'

As Trudy heaved the rubber harness from
my shoulders and fiddled with the straps of

my gown I tuned in to the conversation coming from the next seat.

The lovely Sharon and her client were discussing the men in their lives and it was Sharon's turn.

'I sometimes think my Lloyd's a cycle-path.'

Trudy has a vast collection of Sharonisms and one day she's going to have them bound into a book and present them to her delightful young protégée at an appropriate moment. Lloyd will be absolutely chuffed.

Standing on the pavement outside Trudy's I waited to cross the road – and waited – and waited. It was as though the whole population of Leeds had heard something that we hadn't and were about to apply for sanctuary in Marsh.

The little green man on the traffic lights, who is usually so thoughtful as he guides his pedestrian customers safely across the road, had decided to pack it in for the day and the traffic lights had apparently come out in sympathy. After what seemed a lifetime the endless line of growling cars ground to a juddering halt and we poor stranded souls managed to squeeze our way between the bonnets and the boots until we finally reached the other side of the road.

Our little branch of the HSBC bank was busy as usual, but even so the staff were managing to sort us out at a fair rate of knots. We were paired off in two queues, one lined up at each till, and I found myself parked behind a tiny, birdlike woman of a certain age. In tandem the pair of us stuttered towards the counter and in no time at all she found herself up against the window, face to face with the cashier.

As she conducted her business I pretended that I wasn't really there at all and made a special point of scanning the various posters on the glass security wall, sifting through the rather boring leaflets on the counter and fiddling with the black plastic biro on a chain. Anything rather than have her think that I was in any way listening in to her private transactions.

The cashier made her excuses and left briefly to check on something or other behind the scenes. When she returned the old lady put her mouth as close as she could to the glass and, wiping her hand across her face, she whispered confidentially through her fingers, 'While you were away that woman there...' she nodded discreetly in the direction of the other cashier '...came over and took some money out of your till.'

The first cashier smiled brightly. 'That's quite all right, madam – we both work for the same bank.'

The old lady's body language showed her bitter disappointment at the reaction, but she rallied bravely.

'Well that's as might be – but I'd keep a close eye on her if I were you.'

On my way back home it occurred to me that I get some of my best lines whilst I'm waiting either to spirit my money out of some reluctant cash machine or to kiss it goodbye as it disappears for ever into some welcoming till.

The other day for instance, as I took my turn at the counter in Beattie's kitchenware department, waiting to pay for the set of rubber plate warmers that were going to change my life for ever, I tuned in to the two women in front of me who between them had put together an incredible collection of Lock & Lock plastic food containers.

As the first woman dipped into her purse she smiled at the assistant.

'They spoke very highly of them on QVC the other night.'

Now the QVC shopping channel has changed Aileen's life. With a lorryload of patience and with her forehead pressed up tight against her forty-two-inch television screen she can just about make out the various rings and things through the tiny holes in the lace doily that revolves so slowly in her left eye.

She calls on me every now and then so that I can add the colours and the price and the postage to her fractured picture. In her blank and frustrating world, where a shop window is nothing more than an empty stage, the QVC shopping channel has condensed the high street for her and placed it rather neatly in the corner of her office.

The only problem I have with the channel is that they can never find the slightest fault with anything they have on sale and that isn't the British way of going about things. The presenters have no reservations – everything on offer is so wonderfully, marvellously, supremely, amazingly, out of this worldly fantastic that after just a few moments the urge to throw a brick through the television screen threatens to overpower me and I have to leave the room before I begin to shout, 'It's only a bloody tin opener, for God's sake – it's a tin opener!'

And that would upset Aileen who has learned to ignore the hype and simply glory in the fact that every now and then she can catch the slightest glimpse of whichever little bit of the tin opener happens to be passing her by at that particular moment.

So I get the hell out of there before I feel ashamed of myself.

She was about to open the post as I walked into the kitchen. There was a time when Thermal always met the postman at the gate, walked with him right up to the back door and then insisted on having a good long sniff at each and every envelope before Aileen was allowed to wield her trusty knife.

Nowadays he just can't be bothered. First of all it would involve him in having to wake up and second it would mean leaving the comfort of his radiator for at least a couple of minutes. And who knows, at his age he might never be able to find his way back. Absolutely no point in taking the chance.

'Sorry, Aileen – I'm afraid you're on your own from now on.'

So she has to slit open the unsniffed envelopes without any help whatsoever and then wait for me to read the contents out loud. Today it didn't take long.

I binned the couple that wanted her to combine all her debts into one account and not pay any interest for six months. The offer of a half-price loft conversion went the same way since we don't happen to have a loft, and we somehow managed to resist the combined temptations of the smallest hearing aid on earth and the stair lift.

Most of the advertizing leaflets that wing their way to us these days reinforce my belief that the outside world has the pair of us marked down as a couple of right old codgers. The sales catalogue featuring the latest in winceyette nightdresses and striped pyjamas tended to confirm my suspicions. At least today there was no further news of that blessed walk-in bath that has been snapping at our heels for the past few months or so.

I can never make up my mind about that one. Do the staff at the advertizing agency genuinely believe that older people always take a bath in a one-piece bathing costume or is it that they find the thought of showing the merest glimpse of an ageing body too disgusting for words?

At least we did have one actual letter where the address had been written by hand and a proper stamp had been stuck in the top right-hand corner of the envelope at a slightly wobbly angle as nature intended.

Roy Willett and I go back a long way. For many years we teamed up as a couple of dashing inside forwards for the Chesterfield Nomads football team and our performances improve each time we get together and relive those golden days.

As a footnote to his letter he told me about his mother. She's ninety-five now and still going strong. She rang him and asked him to do this and that for her and not to be so long about it.

'Hang on, Mother – I'm a pensioner myself now, you know.'

She paused for a moment and considered the thought.

'Don't be so ridiculous.'

Apart from Roy's letter the ritual opening

of the post had proved to be something of a disappointment. Aileen enjoys it most when there are one or two cheques involved in the process and even Roy had slipped up there.

She did, however, have one bit of news for me.

'I'd almost forgotten. The vet rang and said that you can pick up Nokia whenever you are ready.'

We considered the prospect for a moment or so and tried to decide whether this was good news or bad news, and we still hadn't made up our minds when I tossed the cat carrier into the boot and reversed the car out of the garage.

As I waited in the reception area at Donaldson's I wondered how my old friend the sick parrot was getting on. This was my third visit and the first time he hadn't been parked on the bench alongside me and I rather missed him.

His owner had said that he was normally a great talker, but he hadn't looked at all well on that last occasion and had been in no mood for idle chit-chat. I asked the receptionist about him and she said that he had been signed off for the time being.

'It's going to be quite a long haul before they get him absolutely right. He isn't exactly in his prime.'

Which reminded me of the baby albatross.

Now he certainly was in his prime and I wondered what had become of him. I was about to ask when a young nurse appeared and relieved me of the wire carrier.

I settled my account and reflected that the two hundred and fifty-odd pounds with which I had just parted worked out at roughly a tenner a scratch over the past year or so and I wondered why the hell I was going to all this trouble. But then the nurse reappeared with the cat basket which now contained Huddersfield's latest contender for the most miserable-looking cat of this or any other year and my heart melted.

'Has he been sedated?'

'No, it's just that he doesn't seem to be interested in anything. I've tried to cheer him up but he's not having any of it.'

We couldn't have this. I was going to have to start all over again and really make it work this time. All it would need was a little give and take on both sides. It's always worked well enough with Tigger and Thermal. I give and they take, but then they do allow me the luxury of thinking of it as a privilege and I'm able to live with that.

The young nurse handed me a slim packet of pills. 'Just one of these a day for twenty days and he should be as right as rain.'

I could see that I might have just the teeniest problem there and took them rather reluctantly. 'OK. I'll give it a go.'

I took the cage from her, apologized for all the trouble Nokia had caused and was about to make for the door when the head nurse Sheila came into the reception area. She would know about the baby albatross.

'Yes, I remember him – he wasn't a real albatross, you know.'

'I rather guessed.'

'He was a very strange-looking chicken. A cross-bred Leghorn, and he's really landed on his feet. One of the nurses took him home and now he's living the life of Riley with five young ladies under his wing, so to speak.'

I was really pleased for the little bird. I love a happy ending, and as I carried Nokia out towards the car I felt a new determination mounting inside me. I must do the same for him.

He hardly moved a muscle all the way home, not even when I had to brake sharply to avoid the young man who raced across the ring road dressed as Danger Mouse.

It's a good job I don't have to write fiction. I don't think I could have made that up in a million years.

Nokia, however, was completely indifferent to the young man and everything else for that matter. He lay on his side and stared straight ahead at the dashboard, not seeming to be aware of anything. He had been so very nervous in the car on his first journey but now it was as though there were no bumps in the road, no noises from the engine, nothing at all in this numb and pointless world of his. I couldn't help wondering if the nurse had been mistaken and he really had been given something to calm him down.

Ever since we drove out of Donaldson's car park I had talked to him non-stop, hoping to cheer him up.

'This car is another type of cat, Nokia. It's called a Jaguar. They are very big cats who live wild in the jungles of Africa. But they aren't lovely and black like you, Nokia – you're more like a puma. They are also very dangerous cats and they live in the jungle as well.'

Maybe it was all my fault. Perhaps I had put him in a coma. I do know I had bored myself absolutely stupid for the last ten minutes or so.

As I pulled up outside the house an extremely ancient drunk came staggering out of the park and across the road. He paused as he passed by my car and then, steadying himself with the help of my offside wing mirror, he took a final swig from his bottle of gin, sadly turned it upside down and shook it just to make sure it was empty, then hurled it over the wall and into my front garden.

I watched it twist and twirl in mid-air as though in slow motion and then heard it smash to pieces as it landed on the paving stones.

'Right.'

I could sort him out, no trouble at all. He stood around about five foot nothing and he must have been well into his seventies.

Now that is my kind of a hooligan. Right up my street. Anything over five foot two and a half and a touch under sixty and I tend to think twice before wading in.

I pushed open the driver's door and went to confront him – but he was nowhere to be seen. He couldn't have made a run for it, could he, not at his age?

He hadn't. He was lying flat on his back by the side of my car and I wondered if he might have banged his head in the fall. I knelt and cushioned him in my arms and as I did so he began to wail.

It was a fearful wail. Maybe his neck was broken? Maybe I shouldn't have moved him? What should I do now?

As it turned out I didn't have to do a thing. He rolled over and grabbed hold of my wrist.

'Yer bastard. Ye're kneeling on me effing knuckles.'

I should have known he wouldn't have hurt himself in the fall. Drunks tend to bounce as they hit the tarmac and as soon as

I backed off his fingers he shot to his feet like a teenager.

He had tears in his eyes as he massaged his hand and I was on the receiving end of a prolonged and extremely inventive stream of expletives. I don't think he repeated himself even once – you had to admire him.

At the same time I like to think that I taught him a lesson that he will never forget. As he limped away back towards the park and I made my way up the path to clear away the glass, I like to think that my natural swagger bore a strong resemblance to that of the late, great, John Wayne.

It wasn't until a little later that I felt rather ashamed of myself. The green gin bottle had exploded all over the path and I had cleared away every last chip of it and tucked them away in the bin before I remembered poor old Nokia, still in his cage on the passenger seat.

As it happened I don't think he even noticed that I had left him alone. He was still deep in his trance and he didn't even blink as I slammed the car door and carried him up the drive. I left him in his cage while I went to check that Thermal and Tigger were going to be well out of the way. He wouldn't want them interfering with him at this early stage of his rehabilitation, but I needn't have bothered.

They were both tucked up comfortably, safe in another world altogether. Laid out on their little sheepskin rugs and butted up in front of their respective radiators, they were each pursuing their own private dreams. Tigger, purring gently in her sleep, seemed to be cuddling something soft and giving, something that wasn't there – maybe the kitten she never had. Thermal, however, was standing no nonsense from anyone as he snarled under his breath, stiffened menacingly and bravely faced up to either a pack of wild rabid dogs or the new Persian kitten from 17a.

Out in the courtyard I carefully laid down the cage so that Nokia could take in the most important landmarks of his old territory – his little house, his kennel and his water fountain, which gushed and bubbled so invitingly.

He never even so much as glanced across at them. I quietly unlatched the cage door and laid it wide open and waited. He showed not the slightest ripple of interest and I thought that perhaps it might be best to leave him to sort out his homecoming in his own good time.

I climbed the steps up to the first floor balcony from where I could keep an eye on him without being seen. I gave him a good ten minutes and in that time he never moved a muscle. It was like watching paint dry.

I had to be more positive if I was going to get anywhere and so I nipped back down, tilted the cage slightly and gently slid him out onto the stone paving slabs. He crumpled and turned through almost a hundred and eighty degrees and I wondered if the vet had removed every single bone in his body along with his testicles – at one point he was almost standing on his head. When he finally came to rest he was flat on his back and facing in exactly the opposite direction and that was when he first noticed the rockery.

Was it possible? He suddenly seemed to realize where he was – could he really have escaped from those awful people and somehow found his way home?

'*Yes!*'

He leapt to his feet, bounded over to the rockery, arched his back and threw his head high in the air as he squatted over the rich black soil and joyously proceeded to crap for England.

I popped down to the cellar and scouted round for the old garden trowel and a fresh plastic bag.

I watched for some time through the kitchen window as he bounded here and there around the courtyard. A short sharp slurp from his little pond followed by a full thirty-five seconds' power nap in his bedroom. A rapid-fire session of guard duty at the entrance to his kennel and then off for another joyous and gloriously relaxed pee on the rockery.

He was home. He'd never thought of it like this before – rather taken it all for granted. Well, never again. No – not ever, ever again would he waste a precious second of his freedom. He was off again, on another full circuit of his courtyard.

The only fly in the ointment was that damned metal prison thing lying still as a corpse in the middle of the yard with its blessed door standing wide open. As he raced here and there happily rediscovering his domain, the moment he came within spitting distance of the cage his whole demeanour would change and he would slope past it fearfully as though it might leap up and grab him. Better get it out of his way and at the same time take him something to eat. He obviously hadn't eaten much at the vet's and he seemed to have lost the odd few grams here and there.

He was still happily chasing around the courtyard as I put a bowl of biscuits down by his kennel, but he froze the moment I began to tidy away the cage.

'It's all right, Nokia. It can't hurt you now.'

He watched intently as I made a great show of storing it out of sight in the dustbin shed and seemed to relax visibly when I slammed the door shut and locked the devilish thing away.

'There you are, Nokey – gone.'

It seemed that a sea change had come over him. He was still nervous and apprehensive now that I was there, but I had never seen him play and frisk around on his own as he had these last few minutes. Could this be the big breakthrough?

I sat on the step by the side of his kennel and muttered encouraging words.

'Well done, Nokia.'

He eyed me suspiciously.

'There's a good boy.'

It's all in the tone, of course – not in the content. I picked up the bowl of biscuits and held them out at arm's length and for a split second he almost came over to me.

I put the dish down.

He sat down.

I pretended not to see him.

He moved closer.

I rubbed my eyes and sneaked a quick glance at him through my fingers.

Even closer.

I looked away.

And then I heard him fall hungrily upon the biscuits as though he hadn't eaten in a week. Which he probably hadn't.

He was all of twenty centimetres away from my left foot now, his black back glistening in the evening light. It must be a sign. He'd never been this trusting before today.

I wondered if I dare just brush my hand briefly across that glossy fur of his. Perhaps this was the moment?

I laid my hand softly on the back of his neck and eased my fingers gently along the length of his spine, before deciding it was time to leave him to his own devices whilst I went and washed away the blood from the three long gashes he'd gouged in my arm.

Why is it that you can never find the Savlon when you need it?

CHAPTER SEVENTEEN

I put down the razor and stared hard at the grizzled old man who stared back at me from the mirror. There's no doubt about it – he wasn't half the man he used to be, which was rather sad because the man he used to be was never really up to much, not even in his prime.

This morning I felt about as useless as one of those towel holders that I had fixed either side of the washbasin. They were a couple of rather attractive gold rings that had looked impressive in the showroom, but in practice they never gave the scrunched up hand towels an even chance to dry themselves off.

I sorted through the more promising of the two in the vain hope that I might eventually come across a virgin strip of towelling that had somehow managed to keep itself to itself, and I had just about given up hope and was reaching out for the bath sheet when my heart performed a perfect three point turn.

A solid lump of aged fur and ancient bones had appeared out of nowhere and crashed against my right ankle. Then an exhausted white cat collapsed across my bare foot.

Thermal must have climbed three flights of stairs to come and tell me what was worrying him and by this time he would have completely forgotten what it was. We are both going downhill fast and this latest trip uphill had really taken it out of him.

I bent and stroked his head. 'What's the matter, my little love?'

As I hovered above him he lay on his back and stared up at my naked bits and pieces, shuddering visibly.

'Put your trousers on first.'

'Sorry – I didn't think.'

It can't have been a very pretty sight from his point of view. I quickly slipped into something loose and then bent down and began to scrub his head once more.

Of course I knew very well what the problem was. Years and years of service in the cat wrangling industry has taught me that one can never hide a single thing from our feline friends.

They seem to sense when a shift in their day-to-day lifestyle is in the offing and this sometimes happens long before I know about it myself. On this occasion, however, Thermal must have smelt the fear that surrounded me yesterday as I steeled myself to break the news to him.

'I was going to tell you.'

'Mmmmm.'

'I was.'

'*Mmmmm.*'

He doesn't actually say '*Mmmmm*' out loud – he says it with his eyes which, whilst the rest of his body has stiffened and slowed down with age, are as sharp and as knowing as they ever were.

'It's only for a couple of days.'

'*How many?*'

'A day or two.'

'*How many?*'

'Well, five actually, but you won't have to go anywhere – Vicky and Neeraj are going to be looking after you. But then you knew that, didn't you?'

Vicky had been round the day before and I'd shown her where we kept their food and who ate what and where they slept and Thermal's eyes had never left her for a moment, which is par for the course with human beings because she's rather good to look at, but Thermal had guessed what was going on.

'It'll make a nice change for you both. You like Vicky, don't you? And did you know that she is a specialist nurse? She works with patients who are in intensive care. And Neeraj is a highly skilled surgeon. His specialty is vascular surgery. So you see you'll be in very good hands if you happen to have one of your funny turns.'

I was fighting a losing battle. Neeraj might be able to remove a patient's gall bladder with one hand whilst stripping out a whole spaghetti junction of varicose veins with the other, but would he know that whenever Thermal loses his favourite ping pong ball it's almost always stuck underneath the electric fire down at the bottom end of the kitchen because that's the way the floor slopes? Of course he wouldn't. And it's this sort of thing that matters to a cat.

As I carried the thoroughly miserable Thermal downstairs he hung lifeless in my arms and sighed theatrically at regular intervals. When I eventually put him down on the hall carpet he would probably start limping. It was a speciality of his and he was at his most convincing when he decided that it was one of his front legs that was playing him up. Whenever he tried it with one of his back legs he looked ridiculous, as though he were attempting a very bad impression of a three-legged Long John Silver. I put him down and he limped off towards the kitchen as though he wasn't long for this world.

It was his front left leg that was broken this time and he was so convincing that for a brief moment I wondered if I should rush him over to Neeraj for immediate surgery.

All this and I still had Tigger's thoughts on the matter to come – best get it over and done with. I plonked myself down between

259

their individual radiators and in a caring and loving manner attempted to appeal to their better natures.

'You remember Nick and Lisa, don't you?'

The cats stared blankly at each other – they must have talked it over and decided that this was a genuine emergency and therefore called for a tactical campaign of non-cooperation.

'You remember when you were a kitten, Thermal, and you were locked in that garage for a fortnight and we looked everywhere but we couldn't find you? Well, when you eventually escaped it was Nick who found you lying half dead in the road.'

'And he's never let me forget it.'

This appealing to their better natures wasn't going very well. I'd forgotten that in times of stress they don't have a better nature, but I carried on.

'Well, they have opened a new restaurant in France and Aileen and I are popping over for a few days next week to have a look at it.'

There were a dozen of us going over to Nice. The Tuesday Club, Aileen's daughter Annie and her husband Martyn, and our friends Chrissie and Robert.

We were all off to celebrate Aileen's birthday in style. It was one of those earth-shattering birthdays that jump out and surprise you every tenth year. I am not allowed to be any more specific than that. It's more than my life's worth – even though she doesn't look it.

I didn't bother telling the cats all this. Much as they love Aileen, they wouldn't have been impressed. Their lives revolve simply around three decent meals a day, a warm comfortable bed and a plentiful supply of liquid that is for ever on tap. We have a lot in common.

I left the inside cats chuntering away miserably to one another and went off to check on the big black one outside. At least I didn't have to worry about Nokia. I had hoped that he might become a little more civilized now that his testicles had branched out and gone off to live a new and challenging life of their own, but he remained just as withdrawn and abrasive as ever.

Vicky would only have to make sure that his dish of Iams was piled high in the mornings and leave it at that. She has the rare gift of being able to make an instant friend of all and sundry, but I'd shown her round a selection of my more accessible battle scars and warned her to give it a miss this time.

I often wish that I could be a normal cat owner. One who goes off on holiday and parks his charges in a cattery for a fortnight or so without a care in the world, knowing full well that, although they might miss him for the first day or two, they would be as right as rain once they had been back at home for a couple of minutes. So what the hell.

Unfortunately I'm not like that – I'm a born worrier. I worry like mad on behalf of my wife, my kids, my friends and my animals and although I have at times taken a deep breath and left my cats in good hands whilst I have upped sticks and flown off on important occasions to New York or Bahrain or wherever, I would really like to have had them each surgically implanted with a very small mobile phone so that I could talk them through any crisis that might arise.

At least I am not alone. Many, many years ago I worked as a freelance broadcaster on Radio Derby and I shared a satellite studio in deepest Matlock with Dave Watson.

Now Dave was a young news reporter who was destined to go far. He was handsome and he had the drive and the talent for the job. He had the contacts and he also had the white raincoat. That very special raincoat that co-starred with every single news reporter in every American movie of the late 1950s, and Dave wore his like a man who was going places.

Then the damned multiple sclerosis invaded his body and took over his life and the last time I saw him was when I happened to be talking at a Derbyshire Police

262

Force annual dinner. He was parked in a wheelchair at a table, being cared for and hand-fed by two officers, one either side of him, all of which didn't stop him being the life and soul of the party.

He is a very brave man and fortunately for him he had had the good sense to marry the lovely Linda who is the sort of person there ought to be more of. She is a born carer and loves and looks after Dave on a non-stop basis twenty-four hours a day, yet still somehow finds time to spoil her four cats outrageously, in addition to playing fairy godmother to the varied assortment of strays who happen to call in to see her on their lonely journey to nowhere in particular.

She has cornered the bed and breakfast market for itinerant moggies simply by trying harder than anyone else. She keeps a kennel out in the garden, complete with a thick woolly blanket, and if the night threatens to turn crisp and icy she nips out and slips a hot water bottle under her rather surprised feline visitor. This often freaks them out, but by the time midnight comes around and the bottle has already been substituted a couple of times with a piping hot replacement, her customers have almost become used to this strange woman and her strange ways and are not particularly surprised when she finally covers them over with a warm fleecy blanket. Should business be rather slack that night then Dave is allowed first use of the blanket.

Linda always cheers me up. After a few minutes of listening to her chatting away happily on the phone, I quietly begin to convince myself that I am just about normal after all.

My only problem in dealing with the reclusive Nokia stemmed from the vet's explicit instruction that, to make sure he recovered completely, I had to give him a small grey pill once every day for the next twenty days.

Luckily they were such tiny little things that I was able to tuck them in amongst his cat biscuits. He would never notice that anything unusual was going on – not in a million years.

What I forgot, however, was that I was dealing with a cat here. At the end of the first day every single biscuit had disappeared – but there sitting quietly in the bottom of his dish was his little round pill.

Thermal had always been an expert at sniffing out unexploded pills and once he had found them he would spit them across the kitchen floor with a look of total contempt on his face.

'You'll have to try harder than that.'

It dawned on me that if Nokia started spitting them all over the place I would never find them out there in the garden and so, since the weather was holding up nicely, I brought his dish into the back porch and left the door propped open.

It took him most of the next day to pluck up the necessary courage to sidle into the porch and then he was off out again in a matter of minutes, but gradually he began to relax and took to having a short nap on the indoor mat mornings and afternoons.

Occasionally I found the odd pill nestling up against the paper bin or lying all on its own at the bottom of his dish, but over the next fortnight I persevered and had only six to go.

He looked a different cat. His eyes were now a fresh leaf green and as clear as a wild mountain stream... I really do apologize. For a whole sentence there I was completely carried away, but I'm sure I'll be all right in a moment. It's just that it was such a pleasure to see him looking so well. Now if only I could persuade him that we were all of us fighting on the same side we might make something of him yet.

That night the Tuesday Club were eating over at Martin and Gillian's house and I was determined to be a brave little chap as the others took turns in taking the mickey out of me.

The week before we were about to have a meal in a rather nice pub and were ordering

the starters chalked up invitingly on a somewhat overcrowded blackboard. I was the
first to come to a decision. I'd have a go at
something new.

'I'll have the redonion soup.'

'The what?'

'The redonion soup.'

There was a noisy silence as the others
scoured the blackboard in a vain search for
this new delicacy. Then there came a joint
cry.

'It's red onion soup, you idiot.'

I tried to point out that on this occasion the
joined-up writing really was joined up, but
they were having none of it and for the
remainder of the evening they redonioned
me into total submission. However, I was
determined to remain dignified and allow the
second wave of redonionization that would
undoubtedly come my way that evening to go
right over the top of my head.

As it happened the soup turned out to be
the least of my worries. My nearside wing
mirror self-destructed on the garage wall as
I reversed the car out through the up and
over door. It would have matched exactly
the offside wing mirror which I had
destroyed only twenty-four hours ago as I
put the car to bed for the night, except that
on that occasion I had also gouged out a
deep line all the way across the passenger
door and the offside wing.

Only the week or so before that I had reversed into a stone wall in a Bakewell car park, and Derbyshire stone walls are not the sort of walls to let you off lightly.

All this after five years without so much as a scratch. I eased the car carefully back into the garage and went to break the news to Aileen.

'We can't go in the car tonight.'

'But I told you only a quarter of an hour ago.'

'Told me what?'

'Paul and Alison are picking us up around half past seven.'

I wasn't quite myself that night – which would have been a blessed relief for all concerned if whoever it was that had taken my place hadn't been such a miserable old devil.

I couldn't help wondering what was happening. My judgement these days was turning into something of a hit and miss affair and the hits were becoming more and more expensive. My memory had long since passed through the 'what on earth have I come upstairs for' stage and was now having great trouble in remembering exactly where it was that we kept the stairs.

As the busy conversation swirled round the table I made a big effort to get back into the swing of things.

For some reason Paul was in the middle of pointing out to Mike that a cat's knees bend backwards and not forwards like those of a human being.

'It's the same with kangaroos.'

Mike had no trouble whatsoever in whipping up a mental picture of the young Skippy as he settled himself down by the side of a billabong, but his mind's eye was obviously having great difficulty in working out the mechanics of a folded-up cat.

I pushed my plate to one side and reached out for my glass of red wine. Then, with a sudden twitch of unerring accuracy, I managed to hurl the whole of its contents down the front of Paul's shirt.

The pity was that for once he was wearing a rather nice shirt. Usually Paul's taste in shirts is such that the majority of them would be greatly improved no matter what substance one decided to throw at them, but that certainly wasn't the case tonight.

'I'm so sorry. I don't know what's the matter with me today.'

'Don't worry about it.'

As everyone buckled down and began to clean up the mess Paul went off with Martin to borrow one of his shirts. By the time he returned, looking even smarter than before, we almost had the place back to normal again.

'I really am sorry.'

'Don't worry. It happens.'

He was dead right – it does. Each week we all turn up with a bottle of wine and tonight Mike and Jean had provided a rather pleasant bottle of Californian Cabernet Sauvignon. I'd seen one just like it in Sainsbury's only the week before. It was lurking on a shelf up at the cheap end and had been reduced to £3.50. My bottle of Shiraz had set me back a staggering £3.99. I just can't see any point in stinting on the little luxuries in life, can you?

I'd parked my freshly refilled glass on the deep white sill of the bay window behind me, well out of harm's way. I turned, picked it up and took a delicate sip, then placed it carefully on the little table mat by the side of my plate. Everyone held their breath for a moment or so as the glass hovered above the mat and then gave me a well-deserved, if somewhat sarcastic, round of applause as it landed safely.

Over by the kitchen door the more confident of Gillian's two cats paused on his way towards his basket. As he sat and contemplated the meaning of life for a few precious moments I watched his knees as they slowly folded themselves backwards. I nudged Mike and pointed him in the direction of the cat.

'There you are.'

Over on the other side of the table a rather smug look began to spread itself across

Paul's face and it was just about to make itself thoroughly at home when for no good reason at all I hurled my second glass of wine all down the front of his shirt.

There are times when apologies count for nothing and this was one of them. To make it worse everyone was being so very nice about it.

Gillian dabbed up the odd spots from the wooden floor and Jean went to work on the polished table with a bunch of paper towels.

'It's hardly anything. Paul soaked up most of it.'

Good old Paul. He had disappeared off stage for yet another dramatic change of gear.

'*When I return, Matthew, I shall be Liza Minnelli.*'

Aileen was still begging someone to please tell her what had happened when he made his second dramatic entrance of the night. This time he had been busy with a pair of kitchen scissors and he sat next to me for the remainder of the evening wearing a shirt especially tailored from a black plastic bin liner – just in case.

At least they had all forgotten about the redonion soup.

CHAPTER EIGHTEEN

Abroad seems to have become a much smaller place than it was since I last set foot in it. There I am strolling through the centre of Nice, having just left the Hotel Grimaldi, on my way towards a quiet cup of coffee with Nick and Lisa in their lovely new restaurant. The mid-morning sun is gently massaging my shoulders and in front of me, strolling arm in arm, are two absolutely stunning young women straight out of a France that is usually reserved for the cinema screen

The two exuded that supreme Gallic arrogance that suggests to the rest of us that we are of little importance, merely extras in a world that revolves entirely around them. Even the locals seemed to be rather over-awed as the women sailed a course straight down the middle of the narrow pavement, obliging all those coming in the opposite direction to either step out into the road or to tuck themselves up against the nearest shop window. ✗

It was as though a twenty-something Brigitte Bardot and a teenage Catherine Deneuve were out on the town together and I wished that Aileen were here with me so that I could share the moment with her.

Earlier this morning I had thrown the heavy bedroom curtains wide open and proceeded to give her a running commentary on everyone and everything that passed beneath our hotel window. It's my privilege in life to be allowed to stand in for her eyes and I was determined that she shouldn't miss out on a thing.

I was still in full flow as she stumbled naked from the bathroom, stared numbly in my general direction and then, in a deep voice thick with sleep, made her current position quite clear to me.

'I'm going to go back to bed now before I wake up and begin to understand what on earth you are talking about.'

So it was just me and the two lovely young women up ahead, who were now turning left into the rue Alphonse Karr. I let them get away for a few moments as I paused to glance in a bookshop window.

I would never dream of admitting to anyone that I might possibly be looking to see if by any chance they had one of my own translations in stock, but this time there wouldn't even be an outside chance.

The publishers in France have never seen fit to buy any of my work and you have to admire their taste. Those in Slovakia have taken a similar line and yet a bookshop in Bratislava threw up a wonderful surprise. The centrepiece of their window display was a huge hardback translation of that well-known English author, Ruth Rendellova.

But in this bookshop window I drew a complete blank and set off again towards the restaurant. The two women must also have been window gazing and were only a few yards ahead of me as they slowed to an elegant halt and Brigitte turned to light a Gauloise for her friend Catherine.

They were just as gorgeous sideways on as they had been from the rear, but I must admit that I rather missed the synchronized wiggling that had entertained me for the past few minutes or so. As I passed them Catherine was explaining something or other to Brigitte and I slowed just in time to hear her broad South Yorkshire accent ring out across this delightful strip of Nice.

'I couldn't let 'im know what'd really 'appened, so I towd 'im it wor a cottonwool-bud related incident– I think 'e got me drift.'

I carried on towards Karrs where Nick and Lisa would be waiting to show me round, but my immediate dreams had just been shattered. Brigitte had thoughtlessly tossed her empty cigarette packet aside and it lay there accusingly on the pavement, the only piece of litter in the entire street.

Sadly they hadn't been smoking Gauloises after all. The discarded pack had once provided a cosy home to twenty Benson & Hedges tipped and its presence on this elegant sidewalk served as a lousy advert for our modern-day Britain.

By the way, what the hell is a cottonwool-bud related incident?

Parked right across from the restaurant was the most wonderful red Ferrari. It must have been at least a week old and it was just about the deepest, reddest deep red Ferrari that I have ever seen in my life.

The top was down and I couldn't resist a closer look. I ran a delicate fingertip across the top of the red leather steering wheel, which seemed to me to be on the wrong side of the vehicle.

I had just noticed that a rather flash bunch of keys had been left dangling from the ignition when a bearded man about the size of a house caught sight of me and came striding across the street shouting something rude in French.

Now since I am a bearded man about the size of a small potting shed I thought it best not to steal the car on this occasion and began to look innocently around me at anything but the car, and it was then that I first caught sight of the magpie.

It was sitting very still on the top of a

man's bald head, who in turn was standing very still on the top of a tall stepladder. Now that's not a sight you come across all that often in Huddersfield and so I moved in for a closer look, just as a beautiful woman in a skimpy red dress and matching shoes walked elegantly out of Nick's restaurant and climbed into the driving seat of the Ferrari.

No sooner had she done so than she climbed out again and strolled back towards the restaurant. She paused at the door for a brief moment to check her wristwatch and as she did so the magpie swooped down, perched on her arm, and in a matter of seconds had ripped off the watch and flown away with it. The woman screamed loudly and scanned the skies above in an attempt to see where the thieving bird had gone.

I could have told her where it was. It was back sitting on top of the head of the bald man who was still standing very still on top of his stepladder, the wristwatch glinting between his fingers. I was surprised she hadn't noticed.

It was at that point that I heard a voice shout 'cut' and saw Nick belting out of the restaurant in order to get to me before the director of the film beat me into a pulp. Apparently they were shooting a television advert for something or other and I wasn't supposed to be in it.

The television company had paid to have the restaurant closed until this evening and Nick took me through to where Lisa was waiting for me at a table in the bar. After injecting me with a quick shot of caffeine they shepherded me into the restaurant proper and showed me round. We had all been here until late last night, fifteen of us seated at a huge table in a raised area that had been curtained off for Aileen's birthday party. I hadn't been able to have a good look over the rest of the place at the time because it had been populated with a host of late-night diners, all at various stages in their evening meal and several at what seemed to be a crucial point in their latest chat-up routine.

But now the kids took me on a pre-lunch guided tour and I was able to see for myself the hard work and imagination that had transformed the place from a dowdy old billiard hall into a sumptuous new restaurant of which they could be well and truly proud.

Afterwards we sat back in the bar and sipped something a little stronger than coffee as we watched the filming from a different angle. Outside, the crew took shot after shot after shot just in case, which is often the sign of a weak director, but on this occasion it was because the actress hadn't quite got her act together – the magpie was word perfect.

Nick explained the plot to me. Apparently, in an attempt to recover her watch the actress would now leap into her Ferrari and chase the thieving magpie all the way down the coast to Monte Carlo. My money was on the magpie.

As we sipped yet another cup of coffee the Tuesday Club began to filter into the restaurant two by two. One pair after another until we almost had a quorum and then the final threesome arrived. Jean and Mike had found a poor lost soul wandering around the hotel.

'He left me all alone.'

'I'm so sorry.'

'He abandoned me. A poor blind woman, all alone in a strange country.'

'Will you ever forgive me?'

'Never – not in a million years.'

'Not even if I bought you a gin and tonic?'

'Oh, go on then.'

Aileen's party last night had more than made up for her fear of flying. It had started in the hotel where she had been given a whole bunch of lovely presents including a large two-seater garden bench from the Tuesday Club.

To save everyone a whole lot of trouble the

actual bench was still cosily tucked up in a flat pack, back in Paul's garden shed in Huddersfield. At this stage in their development the various bits of wood probably had no idea that they were destined to earn their living screwed up tightly together as a piece of garden furniture and they faced a steep learning curve over the next few weeks.

In the meantime a rather distinguished metal plaque had made the journey on their behalf and bore the legend 'Aileen's Bench – with love from The Tuesday Club'.

Outside the restaurant the lunchtime sun was really beginning to flex its muscles and the citizens of Nice were getting the hell out of it. The British, in the shape of yours truly, were in a mind to do exactly the opposite. I took my drink outside and, along with a fair old crowd of assorted tourists, watched as the film unit busily packed their bags.

The actress, despite wearing her spectacular red dress in instalments – just tiny bits and pieces here and there – was receiving far less attention than the magpie, who had turned out to be a real show-stopper. He played it just about right and even allowed himself to be stroked as he posed for photographs, perched on the nervous wrists of his admiring fans.

As I sat and sipped my whisky and water I hoped that I had done the right thing in persuading Aileen to make the journey. She had been very brave. She has a fear of flying which isn't merely a product of her fertile imagination.

Many years ago her left eardrum was badly damaged in an accident, as a result of which the pain of the takeoff stays with her all the way through the flight and is then jacked up a couple of notches as the plane begins its descent. I have only experienced anything like it on one occasion, a quick up and down flight from Liverpool to the Isle of Man, and if I could have opened a window I would have been out like a shot.

Despite all this she had managed, during the past eighteen months, to make it over to Bratislava for her son David's wedding, to New York for the Emmys ceremony and now to France to see Nick and Lisa's new restaurant and celebrate her special birthday.

She had told me a few weeks ago that this really would be the last time she ever flew anywhere, and now that we had only a few hours to go before we boarded the plane home I could see that the tension was beginning to build.

Daughter Annie and our friends in the Tuesday Club knew about this and had made a great effort to steer her mind elsewhere. Alison had unknowingly done her bit late last night.

After dinner she had decided to take a

swim. She didn't have a costume with her but then there was no one about and so she'd whipped off her dress and pants and gone skinny-dipping in the sea. The only thing was, by the time she was ready to come out three German lads had arrived and were sitting on the low wall eating a takeaway.

As Alison emerged from the sea, naked as nature intended, the boys had given her a generous round of applause. She'd taken it all in her stride, as she does her life in general, bowed politely and then slipped elegantly back into her clothes.

She had decided not to tell a soul about it, but when she eventually strolled into the hotel we were all curled up on settees, half asleep and chatting in the lounge. She came over to join us and sat down as though butter wouldn't melt in her mouth – with her hair wringing wet and her dress on back to front and inside out. It did rather give the game away.

We left France bathed in a pool of bright sunshine, but by the time we had passed through customs at Liverpool's John Lennon airport the rain was teeming down and it escorted us along every inch of the M62. The barren moors wore a dark grey overcoat and for once our ears refused to pop as we climbed over the highest chunk of motorway in England.

Huddersfield greeted us rather sullenly, I thought – but then maybe it was just having one of those days. By the time we pulled off the ring road and into Trinity Street it had managed to pull itself together somewhat. Even so, the contrast with the past few days was rather depressing. I couldn't imagine the woman in red racing out of Ali's off-licence and leaping into her waiting Ferrari in order to chase the thieving magpie all the way to Cleckheaton via Brighouse and Heckmondwike.

Then, as I turned off left and was carefully negotiating the last speed bump before home – it can be a little sod when it feels like it and has to be treated with respect – a movement over in the park caught my eye.

An old man in an anorak was cowering on his knees before a tall Zulu warrior who, muscles bulging under his traditional leopard skin, was dancing in a very warlike manner and threatening him with a serious-looking assegai.

I pulled the car up outside the house. 'Got your key, love?'

'Yes.'

'Back in a minute.'

By the time I arrived on the scene the photographer was climbing up off his knees in order to wind up the session.

'Well, thanks a million – I think that went

281

very well, don't you?'

Unlike the South Yorkshire girl in Nice, the Zulu answered in an accent that came all the way up from Oxford via a small private college in Cambridge.

'My pleasure. Give me a little more notice in future and I will make sure to bring a couple of drummer friends with me.'

It was with a spring in my step that I strode back to the car and began to pull the luggage from the boot. Good old Huddersfield. After a rather dodgy start it had managed to get its act together and come up with a winner.

Aileen had managed to make it no further than the inner hallway and as I pushed open the door I tripped over her foot. She was lying full length on the carpet and the inevitable flutter of panic began its little dance in my stomach, until I saw that she had both arms wrapped round an ancient white cat who could have been purring for England.

'Make a fuss of Tigger, love. I fell over her as I came through the door.'

Under the hall table an equally ancient and now thoroughly miserable old tortoiseshell was putting on an exhibition of semi-professional sulking that had to be seen to be believed.

'Out you come, Tigger. Come on, sweetheart – now tell me all about it.'

I knelt and prised the patient out from under the table, then carried her through to the kitchen and sat her on my knee.

'Now where does it hurt?'

Apparently it hurt all over, but the worst of it was, her feelings had been badly bruised. She had been really excited as she came out into the hall to welcome us, but Aileen had only managed to locate Thermal and had trodden on her tail.

'*And my paw.*'

'She didn't mean to. She can't see you, Tigger – you should know that by now.'

'*Well, it hurt.*'

There was a time when Tigger would sway like a matador and slip out of the path of Aileen's oncoming feet at the very last second, but she hadn't done much swaying and slipping these past few years since the dreaded arthritis had taken hold of her muscles and tied them into knots.

Aileen joined us in the kitchen wearing Thermal round her neck at a rather rakish angle. He hadn't been this far up off the ground for some time now and his face was white as a sheet – but then I suppose it always has been.

He eased forward a little and nuzzled Aileen on the nose. We hadn't been made so welcome for years. Usually when we return from a spell away they'll have nothing to do with us for hours – not until they need feeding, and then they tend to let us off the hook.

Vicky and Neeraj must have been a huge success as cat sitters. Either that or they had threatened them with grievous bodily harm if they squealed.

I made a pot of coffee and for another five minutes or so we enjoyed the full attention of our two furry old-age pensioners. Then their eyes began to droop and their ancient fur went all limp and they decided that enough was enough and sloped off to the comforting warmth of their respective radiators.

Amongst the mail lying on the floor in the back porch was a card telling us that the postman had left a parcel out in the bin shed. I pulled open the back door to go and retrieve it and as I did so Nokia, who must have been leaning against the outside of the door, fell inside and landed right across my foot.

My ankle panicked a few seconds before I did, but the rest of me soon caught up with it and together we danced backward out of range. Nokia had already panicked and was standing to attention out in the courtyard.

That was the very first time that he hadn't lashed out the moment I had come within clawing distance. Maybe it was simply because he had been taken by surprise – or could it be that losing his bits and pieces had actually made a man of him?

His eyes were a revelation, no longer a pair of evil-looking slits that would have had him picked out time after time in a police line-up.

'That's the cat, officer – I'd know him anywhere.'

No longer weeping and all gummed up, they were a wonderful bright green, beautifully round and innocent. His coat had been recently polished and he looked every inch the sort of young man you could take home to meet your mother.

I sat down on the step and beckoned to him.

'Come on, Nokia.'

He stood his ground. He wasn't ready for that sort of thing.

'Come on, Nokes.'

He sat down and began to lick his bum. I tried appealing to his better nature.

'Come on, you daft prat – I won't hurt you.'

He ignored me. He'd found something very interesting in his nether regions and I was just about to tell him to go and get stuffed when Aileen came into the porch and kicked me viciously in the small of the back.

I apologized immediately, of course. I find it saves a lot of time in the long run and my apology was accepted with good grace.

'Sorry.'

'That really hurt my toe.'

'Sorry, love. Sometimes I just don't think.'

She carried on out into the courtyard to have a look round. She knows exactly where everything is. The various perfumes of the oriental lilies are on duty to warn her that she is now approaching the edge of the lower terrace and needs to take a step upward. On the odd occasion her timing is a little too previous and then it looks as though she is auditioning for John Cleese's Ministry of Silly Walks, although of course we would never dream of telling her.

Movable objects, however, are a different kettle of fish.

'Nokia's on your right by the fountain.'

'Come on then, Nokes. Let's go and have a sniff at the hanging basket.'

To my surprise he rose to his feet and followed her. Then waited until she had settled herself on the old garden bench, gave it a few moments and quietly parked himself about a couple of feet away.

'He's just to your left.'

She leaned over towards him.

'We're having a brand new bench soon, Nokia. It's going to go in that corner over there.' Paul was to put together the bench as soon as possible and then we were having a get-together to screw on the plaque.

Nokia nodded knowingly and sat back like

a penguin, furking about in his undercarriage. I was on my way out to join them when Aileen rose to her feet and began to march straight towards him.

'Stop!'

She stopped dead, a couple of inches away from those lethal paws. His back had arched, his claws were fully loaded. Then he must have decided that she just wasn't worth it and he tucked his claws back in their holster and sloped off down the path.

I took her arm. 'That was close.'

She smiled. 'Give me a week or so and I'll have him eating out of my hand.'

CHAPTER NINETEEN

Whenever we have been away for a while I see the house through a fresh pair of eyes. I really miss being here and it's always good to be back again. It's been a very happy home for both of us and we love it to bits and every time we return to it I look around as though I've never seen it before.

Today the wooden rack that hangs high above the kitchen table caught my eye as the sun sparkled and glinted from the business-like butcher's hooks, the stainless steel pans and the most enormous spider's web that I have come across in many a year.

You could have landed a shoal of mackerel with that web, and I wondered how long it had been up there. I plonked Tigger down on the floor and climbed up on the table for a closer inspection. It was not only an exhibition of great engineering, it was an absolute work of art by a spider who certainly knew what he was about.

He couldn't have created this in the few days we spent over in France, not unless he'd taken on a couple of lads and been training them up. It must have been here for ages and I couldn't imagine how I had failed to notice it before. For a moment I wavered. It was so beautiful that I wondered if I should consider it as a feature, do away with the butcher's hooks and hang all the pans from it. Be a great talking point.

No, that would be ridiculous. Without further ado I reached out and yanked the silky threads away from their moorings. As I did so I noticed a movement on top of that square box thing. The black square box thing that powers the light in each of the four corners of the overhead wooden rack thing and brings them bouncing into life. I do hope I'm not being too technical for you.

I froze and waited to see if it was what I thought it was – and it was. After a couple of minutes of extra time, just to make sure he was safe, a rather dejected spider emerged and surveyed the devastation that I had brought about with a mere flick of the wrist.

I have seen a lot of spiders in my time but never one who looked as miserable as this poor little chap. He had a tear in the corner of his eye. He glared at me with his other eye.

'*You bastard. Have you any idea what you've gone and done? I began that when I was just starting out, when I was only a bit of a kid and had all that surplus energy. I couldn't do it now.*'

He let out a racking sob, then quickly pulled himself together. I was devastated.

'I'm so sorry. Look – I'll help you build another one, somewhere safe. The meter room in the cellar would be really good; hardly anyone ever goes in there.'

He moved in towards the wreckage for a closer look and as he did I noticed that he suffered from a rather nasty limp, probably brought about by having a couple of his legs missing. He turned and glared at me again.

'If I'd wanted it somewhere else I would have built it somewhere else, wouldn't I? You people will never understand. It's not just a fly-related thing, it's a whole way of life.'

He broke down again, tiny spider-sobs racking his thin little body – or maybe I just imagined that. Yes, on second thoughts I think I must have imagined that last bit.

I couldn't bear to witness his suffering any longer and so I jumped down from the table and just missed landing on Aileen as she came in to have her nails touched up.

Once a fortnight Francine comes over and gives them a right professional seeing to and they look absolutely wonderful, but then, as the varnish chips and fades in the run-up to her next visit, I am often called upon to render first aid.

There was a time when I thought of myself as playing the role of Antony to Aileen's Cleopatra. Nowadays I seem to have been cast as a sort of Parker to her Lady Penelope.

'What can I do for you, ma'am?'

She sat down and plonked some bottles of nail varnish on the table in front of me.

'What shade is that?'

I turned it upside down, squinted, then closed one eye. 'Mat – Adore – Red.'

'And that one?'

'Marooned – on – the – Subway.'

'That one?'

'Russian – to – a – Party.'

'Must be that one then.'

'Grand – Central – Carnation?'

'That's the one.'

I eased my chair into position beside her, opened the bottle of Grand-Central-Carnation and prepared to repair Francine's original work of art.

'Plonk your fingers down there.'

'Down where?'

'In my hand.'

'Where's your hand?'

Even after all these years I still forget every now and then.

I started on her left little finger nail. It tends not to get itself involved in her day-to-day activities as much as the rest of the team and so it makes for a good practice start.

I cracked on. One thing I've learned about painting nails is that you have to show them that you are not afraid. Once you begin to have doubts and hesitate they finish up looking like a corrugated roof. The fact is that I'm petrified of painting her nails – but

I'm a very good actor.

I hung her left hand out to dry and reached for the other one. She pulled it away.

'I'm going to sneeze.'

Nail varnish always sets her off.

'Atishoo.'

'Bless you.'

'Atishoo.'

'Bless you.'

She is the only person I have ever known who actually says 'Atishoo' when she sneezes. Perhaps it has something to do with her once being an English teacher in a girls' grammar school.

She hung her nails out to dry and I gave a huge sigh of relief. I'd painted a little more of her ring finger than I was supposed to and it looked as though I'd become a little blasé by the time I had worked my way round to her right thumb, but on the whole they looked pretty good to me.

I had been rather worried when I first put varnish to cuticle this morning because I hadn't been let loose on her nails since I had woken up a few days ago and found that I had a map of Wales stuck in the middle of my right eye.

Not a complete map. It went down as far as Swansea and Cardiff and then across as far as Haverfordwest, but only up as far as Machynlleth, which meant that I was denied the delights of both Wrexham and

Betws-y-Coed.

It had been early on Saturday morning when it first appeared and frightened the life out of me. The hospital emergency department seemed to be the only place open to me at the weekend.

I had popped in there just the other week with another problem and they had been wonderful. They had whipped me away from all the drunks and the druggies and I had spent that night and all the next day tucked up in a cosy ward, having test after test after test.

I realized that there wouldn't be all that many drunks around this early on a Saturday morning, but all the same I didn't really fancy it and what's more I couldn't afford to be kept in. Aileen needed me close at hand and I also had a joint of beef in the fridge that would self-destruct if I didn't get it into the oven by lunchtime.

So as soon as they opened I nipped down to Vision Express to have my eyes tested and by the time they ushered me upstairs the map of Wales had slipped slightly over to one side and Haverfordwest had magically disappeared into the Irish Sea.

Nigel usually takes care of me but he was busy tormenting some other poor soul at the time and my case was assigned to the lovely Sanghita, who really came up trumps.

She examined me very carefully, brought Nigel in for a second opinion and then rang a consultant at the hospital.

'Tell him to ring for an appointment next week.'

She took a deep breath and steeled herself for an argument. 'No. I think you should see him today.'

Sanghita was determined not to be bullied into settling for second best and they agreed to see me over in Halifax early the next morning, which just happened to be a Sunday.

I do hope that I let Sanghita know how grateful I was as I said goodbye and left her to go home and set fire to my long-suffering joint of beef.

On the way home I popped into Sainsbury's. Wouldn't take more than a couple of minutes, I thought. Needed to top up on the vegetable front and collect the odd item here and there. In and out in no time at all.

It wasn't until I found that I was simply wandering round the store looking at the bath towels and raffia waste-paper baskets that I realized that something was not quite right with me. I needed to get down on my knees, right now before I fell over, and so I did. In the middle of an aisle, with a stack of velvet cushions on my right and... I have no idea what was on my left.

I stared at the floor. It's a sort of brown mosaic pattern that matched my trousers perfectly. I'd never noticed that before. A woman hesitated by my side. Her husband pulled her away.

'Leave him. He's drunk.'

I wish.

My head was beginning to clear, but it still had some way to go. A young woman talking loudly into a mobile phone swayed around me without missing a beat and a woman with a pram purposefully looked the other way as she manoeuvred her offspring around my head.

This wasn't the Huddersfield I'd come to know and love.

'Are you all right, lovey?'

Now that was.

'Here, get these underneath you.'

A young woman with a toddler had taken a bunch of the gold velvet cushions from the shelf and was trying to ram them under my head and under my knees. The toddler was toddling back from the fixture with fresh supplies.

'No, really. I think I'm coming out of it now.'

'Are you sure?'

'Mmmmm.'

'You take it easy then.'

I very carefully eased myself into what almost passed for an upright position, not quite knowing what to expect. The young woman knelt down, stuck her hip hard up against mine and put her arm round me as she helped me from my knees. This business of passing out does have its compensations.

She rapped out an order to her daughter. 'Get them back on 'shelf.'

The toddler obeyed instantly and staggered over to the display with a huge pile of cushions.

I managed to steady myself on my feet. 'Thank you so much.'

'You going to be all right?'

'I'll be fine.'

'You're not driving, are you?'

I shook my head. 'No.'

'Good job.'

Well, not just yet anyway.

She saw me over to the restaurant before she said goodbye and then I went in search of a table, thankful that I had a trolley to lean on. You can't lean on a basket, they're not built for it.

I sat at a table for some time, waiting for my head to clear and for my legs to come to their senses. Eventually I managed to persuade them to take me over to the coffee machine. They weren't too keen on the idea at first but after a damn good talking to they reluctantly agreed.

A waitress spotted me staring at the

contraption, trying to make sense of the instructions. This time they were in Hungarian or some other such language and I was surprised that everyone else seemed to be having no trouble whatsoever. She came over.

'Big 'un or little 'un?'

'Big 'un.'

'Black or white?'

'Black.'

'Where are you sitting?'

'Over there.'

'Come on.'

She sat me down with the coffee and took my money.

'Keep the change.'

'Don't be so daft.'

I sat for a while with my eyes closed, but that only made me feel worse so I reached out and tried to pick up my mug of coffee, but the handle was missing. The waitress had been very kind, but fancy giving me a mug without a handle.

I glanced across at the family seated at the next table. They had handles on their mugs. The little kid in the high chair had two handles on his. Perhaps he'd pinched mine when I wasn't looking. Kids these days, they want locking up. Then, merely by chance, I came across my handle. Somebody had gone and stuck it on the other side of the mug.

After a while my head began to clear and I scrapped the idea of asking one of the Tuesday Club if they would mind coming over to pick me up. Give it a few more minutes and maybe another coffee.

I was just about to go over and give the machine another chance when a middle-aged woman came charging out of the smoking section with all guns blazing. She faced up to the assistant behind the till and pointed back whence she came.

'There's a woman sitting at that table over there and she's not smoking.'

The assistant couldn't have been trained to deal with emergencies like this, but she coped admirably.

'Which woman?'

'That one over there.'

The guilty woman was quite oblivious of the fact that she'd just been pointed out by the quivering finger of indignation and carried on reading her book, taking the odd sip of her coffee, nibbling at her sandwich.

'She's still eating.'

'Not the point.'

'Yes it is.'

'She hasn't even bothered to get herself an ashtray, has she? And where are her fags? Can you see her fags?'

I looked round the smokers' den and, apart from the table in question, there wasn't another without its glass ashtray and its packet of cigarettes, snuggled up cosily to a plastic lighter.

'She's no smoker.'

The assistant, now realizing she was dealing with a professional, slipped out from behind the till.

'I'll go and have a word with her.'

The would-be smoker reached over the till, picked up a glass ashtray, stuffed her cigarettes and lighter inside it ready for the off, then, clutching them to her breast, waited to see what would happen over in the promised land.

The young lady listened very carefully and then, collecting together her bits and pieces, jumped up immediately and moved towards another table. She smiled across at the complainant.

'I'm so sorry – I had no idea.'

The smoker scowled. 'I'll bet she bloody didn't. They're all the same, that bloody lot. Butter wouldn't bloody melt. She's lucky she didn't get a thick ear.'

At one time I used to smoke around thirty cigarettes a day. They relax you, you know.

I circled the car park three or four times before passing myself fit to venture out on the road. It's an enormous car park and it must have cost me at least a couple of quid in fuel. This being a conscientious citizen can be a very expensive business.

Paul was waiting for me when I arrived home. He'd bought a baguette and a coffee from Jazz Cuisine on his way over and was trying to relax and enjoy them as he sprawled across Aileen's bench. He would have made a much better job of relaxing if Nokia hadn't been staring at him from the other seat.

The Tuesday Club had delivered Aileen's birthday present in person the day before, each of them with a bit of this and a bit of that tucked under an arm. Paul had assembled the whole bag of tricks whilst the rest of us just stood around and had a drink of this and a drink of that. Being the one who can do practically everything must be rather a pain at times.

He eventually brought the whole thing together, making a huge presentation of screwing the stainless steel plaque into place. We applauded long and loud and even Jean broke off from talking about her mother to join in.

As soon as seemed appropriate I eased Jean back into her narrative. She was telling us about moving her vulnerable and aged mother into a small bungalow where it seemed she would have more chance of coping with the day-to-day business of life. The old lady hadn't been able to use the stairs for some time and the bungalow in question happened to be right next door to where she already lived, so when it came onto the market they snapped it up. Jean's mother wouldn't have the problem of getting used to new surroundings.

An old man had lived there on his own for years and the place was in a sorry state. They cleaned it from top to bottom, decorated throughout and turned an ancient coalhole into a laundry room. Since there was hardly any kitchen to speak of they had scrapped what there was and started all over again. Together with Jean's brother and her son David, they had fitted it out with a series of brand new units, all designed to make life easy for a woman with mobility problems, and then they had held their breath and hoped that they had thought of everything. As a final touch they arranged for care workers to call in four times a day to do this and that and generally keep an eye on things.

She would be fine, Jean's mother told them, they mustn't go worrying about her all the time. And then, as they eventually settled her in and were leaving, she had a final question for them.

'How will I know when I'm hungry?'

Later that week Jean had called to take her shopping, and as they locked the front door behind them her mother turned and cast an eye over her strange new home.

'Who is it that lives here when I'm not here?'

I wish my mother had known her. They would have got on like a house on fire.

Paul reached to take his coffee from the built-in table that divided man and cat. Nokia shifted slightly nearer to him and coiled his lithe black body as though ready to strike. Paul decided that his coffee would probably be too hot anyway. He'd leave it there to cool for a while.

For all the wariness, the two seemed to have a genuine respect for each other and maybe if I could persuade them to go away for a weekend together, paint-balling or white-water rafting or something manly like that, then they might bond and become lifelong friends.

As it was Paul disappeared into the house to size up for a new shower in the top floor bathroom and Nokia nipped into the shrubbery for a quick pee.

CHAPTER TWENTY

Strolling back down the hill from Marsh. Just had my hair cut and my eyebrows trimmed. Trudy always insists on the eyebrows and I never argue with Trudy. Heard the latest from the lovely Sharon.

'When I die I want to be cremated and then have my body left to medical science.'

I bet medical science can hardly wait.

I called in to buy Lisa a birthday card from Don't Forget. Alison told me about this morning's attempted bank robbery. Apparently it hadn't been as well organized as the previous attempt.

At least ten people waiting at the bus stop had seen the man put his foot through a temporary panel in the front door, drop down on his knees and crawl inside our local branch of Lloyd's. It only opens for business a couple of days a week and they obviously don't go throwing money about when it comes to security.

Several passengers on the bus bound for Lindley were fishing mobile phones from their pockets and handbags. Car drivers waiting at the pedestrian crossing had their phones glued to their ears and now the intercom between the local shops had brought all the traders out onto the street. Alison immediately popped back into Don't Forget and dialled the police.

'We've heard, love – we've had over thirty calls already. They're on their way.'

Apparently the second barrier is an automatic door and it had very politely stepped to one side and welcomed the would-be thief with open arms. Passersby knelt down on the pavement, peered through the hole in the door and began a running commentary

'He's sitting down. He's reading something. He's just about to...'

A police car screeched to a grinding halt and a couple of policeman poured out.

'Right – everyone out of the way. Stand well clear – leave this to us – we'll deal with this.'

They spread themselves face down on the pavement, peered in through the hole in the door and issued a series of warnings that came straight out of the latest instalment of *The Bill*.

There was no answer.

'Right. We're coming in.'

The two crawled in through the hole and disappeared. For quite a while there was complete silence. The crowd waited with bated breath and then out came the two policemen, dragging the would-be thief by his legs.

He offered no resistance. He just lay there on the pavement, clutching a mortgage application form in his hot little hand.

Frankly I don't rate his chances all that highly.

As I reached home and turned in through the front gate I saw that a couple of geriatric cats were catnapping on the front step. It's what they do best these days. Thermal's head seemed to have sunk deep into the stone paver and Tigger's bum was pressed up hard against Thermal's. It's what they call togetherness.

As I closed in on them I could hear the deep breathing and see their wheezy little chests rising and falling in unison. It was about the most exercise they had managed all week.

I could also see a sleek black bum sticking out from behind the large sand-coloured plant pot that is home to a lonely and heart-broken hydrangea. Up until a fortnight ago he had a friend. We had two identical hydrangeas, one standing either side of the front door, and visitors often commented on them. Then one day a miserable excuse for a thief nipped up the path in broad daylight and made off with the more vulnerable of the two. Nowadays we have to make do with just the one and Aileen calls him the Lone Hydranger.

The sleek black bum must have heard someone approaching and it very carefully hitched itself up tight behind the plant pot, well out of sight. Unfortunately it seemed to have forgotten that it was attached at the other end to a thick black tail which rather gave the game away.

I peeped over the top of the hydrangea and looked down on the crouching Nokia. He didn't see me, but what I saw wasn't at all the vicious feral cat that had roamed around the courtyard for the past year or so. Instead, a young and rather innocent cat now stared at Thermal and Tigger with lonely eyes that ached for companionship.

'I wish I could think of something to say to them.'

He eased a little closer.

'What if I just said hello and left it at that?'

He braced himself.

'They couldn't object to that, could they?'

He took a deep breath.

'Hi.'

Tigger was the first to react – she fell off the step.

'Bloody hell fire!'

She doesn't normally swear like that and I think we can turn a blind eye on this occasion. Ten years ago she would have had him for breakfast, but that was then and this is now and she flew off down the path like greased lightning, with a dozy, half-asleep Thermal hard on her heels.

When I say they flew off like greased lightning, you must realize that I am talking about lightning that has gone off somewhat. Lightning that is surplus to requirements. Lightning that is a long way past its sell-by date. Even so, they moved quicker than either of them had done in the last few years.

'Hard luck, Nokes.'

As soon as he saw me peering down on him his back arched, his hair stood on end and he was no longer the vulnerable young cat I fancied I'd stumbled across a few moments ago. He glared at me, then turned and stalked off up the path towards his house in the courtyard.

I turned in the opposite direction and went off to provide counselling for a couple of old-age pensioners who had been all shook up by the confrontation and would be absolutely stiff as a board in the morning.

I fixed a simple lunch for Aileen and myself. Later that afternoon I was to report to the Royal Infirmary for an MRI scan on my neck. Earlier that morning I had once again been over to the hospital in Halifax with my right eye. I thought it best if the two of us went together.

The map of Wales had slimmed down somewhat and magically reinvented itself as the Isle of Wight. It made for a pleasant change and gave me a chance to visit Shanklin once again, bringing back many happy memories of my honeymoon there with Diana. First thing tomorrow, by popular demand, my heart and I were booked to appear for a return engagement at the Royal Infirmary

To be honest I was more than a little worried about whatever it was that was happening to me. From early in the year 2000 until late in 2005 I hadn't been at all well. I felt absolutely lousy and by lunchtime each day I was completely exhausted and ready for bed.

I could do little more than take care of Aileen and the six years simply passed by as though they had never been anywhere near the place. I managed to produce the first two pages of a new book and then found that I couldn't continue and had to release it back into the wild.

Eventually the medical profession sorted me out and I tentatively started work on a little something I provisionally called *Paws in the Proceedings*. I had just completed chapter one and hated to think that those wasted years might repeat themselves all over again. I didn't want this book to fizzle out. I needed to get back to work and also the money would come in rather handy.

I found there were two distinct sides to this business of passing out in company. On the frightening side were those occasions such as the night I was being paid to entertain the Rotary Club of Hull. Ten minutes into my allotted hour I felt my head break loose from its moorings and then I heard myself saying from quite a distance away, 'I'm sorry. I don't think I can...'

Then, after collapsing backwards and smashing a chair in the process, I spent that night and most of the next day tucked up in Hull's Royal Infirmary

On the not so worrying side were those more organized occasions at home as I sat having a meal with Aileen. She would be happily chatting away on the other side of the kitchen table when I would feel myself beginning to slide away into another world.

It happened so often these days that I had it down to a fine art. At the first warning I would gently fold myself down onto the floor, pass out for a while, come round in my own time and then lie very still on the carpet until my head decided to give me the all clear.

When I took a deep breath and shakily eased myself back onto my chair, I would often find that Aileen was still carrying on with whatever it was she was talking about, having not the slightest inkling that I'd left her all on her own for a few minutes.

'So do you think we should or shall we forget about it until the weather sorts itself out?'

I had no idea what she was talking about. I would have to play this one by ear.

'How much will it cost?'

She wasn't quite sure. 'Well, they don't come cheap, do they?'

'Then let's leave it until the weather sorts itself out.'

She had a little think. 'Perhaps you're right.'

Phew! That was close.

As soon as I plonked myself down in the hospital waiting room I knew that it was going to be a good day. Without having to go searching through pile after pile of tatty magazines on table after table, I came across a fresh-faced copy of *Woman and Home* dated March 2002. It was sitting there right by my side, just asking for it.

In all my visits over the past few years I had never found a magazine as up to date as this and I happily settled down to work my way through it page by page. The horoscopes were a few years out of date, but the recipe for baked apple strudel with a tart lemon sauce had more than stood the test of time and I thought I might try it out on Aileen when I got home.

I was just wondering how I could tear out

the recipe without anyone noticing when a pregnant young girl, barely out of school, wearing a crop top and low-cut jeans came and plonked herself down beside me.

She was tiny but her belly was enormous. It flopped out over the straining denim and was the perfect setting for a navel that had ballooned up into a scale model of Mount Vesuvius. It looked as though it might erupt at any moment.

The navel actually seemed to be moving about and I couldn't take my eyes off it. Maybe the baby was unscrewing it from the inside. Perhaps it had decided to make a break for it and thought it had come across an emergency exit in the roof.

The girl gave an almighty groan. She was far too young to be going through all this.

'Are you all right?'

She stared at me as though I was from another planet.

'Ugh.'

I felt very sorry for the poor little unborn child. It's not the greatest start in life to have a mother who is not only as thick as two short planks but still has to work her way through those horrible teenage years.

A voice called out from across the room.

'Deric Longden.'

A nurse beckoned me to follow her, but I was only just out of my seat when the young girl's voice stopped me in my tracks.

311

'Excuse me, but are you Deric Longden the writer?'

'Yes, that's right.'

'Oh, I love your books. *The Cat Who Came In From The Cold* was the very first book I ever read.'

'Well, thank you very much. You're very kind.'

She smiled and her blank face suddenly looked quite beautiful.

'I can't wait to tell my mother I met you. She'll be thrilled.'

As I followed the nurse out of the room and on down a long corridor I had quite a spring in my step. Most people would have taken one look at that pregnant young girl and jumped to all the wrong conclusions.

I am glad I'm not like that.

As I lay all trussed up in the submarine-like scanner with my head fastened inside a small white cage, I tried hard not to listen to Radio 2. The powers that be had invited me to bring my favourite music along with me, which was very thoughtful of them, but I planned to take advantage of the solitude and think beautiful thoughts.

They said that would be fine but did I realize that there would be a fair amount of noise in there? I hadn't, but I certainly did now and was almost pleased when Radio 2 snuck inside the headphones whilst no one was looking.

The pleasure didn't take long to wear off. I am allergic to disc jockeys. I couldn't do anything about the radio and so I tried to switch myself off instead by reliving a story Nick told me some time ago. Maybe it was the medical connection that had brought it to mind. Might be able to use it some time.

He and Lisa had flown off to St Lucia for a well-earned holiday, looking forward to slowing down their life to a gentle trot as they relaxed under the Caribbean sun. Unfortunately Nick had no option other than to take his dodgy back along with him.

His back has been an absolute pain in the neck for years and the long flight did it no favours whatsoever. By the time they reached the hotel he could barely walk. Once in the room he stretched out on the bed to try to ease the pain and then found he couldn't move.

Lisa phoned the hotel doctor who was with them in no time at all. An elegantly suited Jamaican, he took one look at Nick and handed him four large pills.

'Here, man, take one of these straight away.'

Nick did as he was told and immediately passed out. He was in another world for over ten hours, which is a long time to keep an eye on yourself as you float just underneath the bedroom ceiling.

When he came to he was completely free from pain, his movements were unrestricted and he felt better than he had done for years. The two weeks went by like a dream and the day before they were due to fly back home the doctor called in to see them.

They thanked him profusely.

'Hey – my pleasure, man. Just wanted to know if you had any of dem pills about your person?'

'No – I took the lot.'

'No problem, man. I just didn't want you taking 'em back through customs. Only they doan't understand, you know.'

By the time I arrived back home the A team were already at work, trying to make the house look as though it had just stepped out of the shower. They don't usually arrive on the same day like this, but what the hell – the more the merrier.

I don't know what I would do without them. The window cleaner doubles as my financial adviser. He studies the business sections of all the leading papers and juggles his own portfolio with consummate skill. He knows what is hot and what is not.

'The secret is knowing when to sell.'

Maria and Kate arrive courtesy of Merry Maids and know everything there is to know about everything. Besides giving the house a good seeing to they have recently program-med the new DVD player for me and sorted out the long-running problem I have been having with my chips – apparently I hadn't been drying them off properly before pop-ping them into the deep fat fryer. They have also taught me the most effective way of removing cat hairs from the lounge carpet – you have to shuffle backwards, scuffing the soles of your shoes across the pile as you go.

Not long ago Maria took our tempera-mental vacuum cleaner to pieces and cleared a blockage by blowing down the business end of one of the tubes. A huge tangled knot of goodness knows what flew out like a bullet and almost took Thermal's head off. It certainly showed young Dyson who's the boss round here and he's been on his best behaviour ever since – he hasn't rung in sick or anything once.

As my memory is deteriorating at a rate of knots I thought it might be a good idea to make a note of their various technical and domestic tips. They might come in rather handy over the next few years, so I jotted them down in a notebook – things like which buttons on the remote control I should press in order to persuade the pictures from the security cameras to appear on the television screen. ✗

It all worked rather well for a week or so but now I can't remember what on earth

I've done with the book and so it's back to square one. I know I put it down somewhere.

I had to step over young Dyson as I made my way up to see Aileen. Maria had him in a death lock. He smiled up at me bravely.

'*Help.*'

I thought it best to keep well out of it and carried on. Aileen was just on her way out of her office.

'There's something that sounds large and unimaginable flying around in there.'

'You leave this to me, my little one.'

I strode manfully past her and opened up the cupboard where we keep all our personal stationery, together with six weeks' supply of Trebor's extra strong mints and a yellow plastic fly swatter, just in case.

I stow fly swatters all over the house. When you live on four floors you can't be doing with racing up and down stairs as though you're not right in the head so I buy them in bunches and spread them around.

I will happily spend a good half an hour trying to rescue a spider from the bath and I always apologize profusely to the elderly razor blade that I am about to replace with a much younger model ('Look, it's nothing personal. If I had my way...') but I just can't be doing with wasps and flies and if they invade my space they must suffer the consequences. My batting average has always been pretty good but it has improved enormously since the day someone told me that house flies always take off backwards.

Compared to flies, wasps are a piece of cake and this one had really let himself go. He was breathing heavily. He'd obviously put on a lot of weight recently and his stripes didn't quite meet round the middle.

I sorted him out and then went and told Aileen that it was safe for her to return to her computer. She gave me a kiss.

'My hero.'

I accompanied her back into her office on the off chance that I might get another one.

'How did you go on at the hospital?'

'Fine. It was a bit noisy in the scanner, but no problem at all – they reckon I'll live.'

She told her computer to wake up. It yawned and had a really good stretch.

'You have mail.'

She ignored it.

'You'd better live. You can't go leaving me on my own. Me – a poor blind woman with six children to bring up.'

Leaving aside the fact that our kids no longer need to be changed or breastfed on a regular basis, mainly due to the fact that there isn't one of them under forty years old, she had touched on a nagging worry that refuses to leave me alone for any length of time.

We rarely speak of it, but it's always there.

'I can't leave you. I only restocked the freezer on Wednesday.'

'Well, that's taken a weight off my mind – especially since the Tuesday Club are coming here tonight.'

'Oh my God – I'd forgotten.'

'Thought you had.'

'Better go and raid the freezer.' I gave her a kiss and made to leave.

'There's just one other little thing you can do for me, if you don't mind.'

She whipped off her top, wrapped her arms tight around me and began to whisper in my ear.

I went all weak at the knees.

'Now can you see why you can't leave me on my own?'

I certainly could and so I gave her a great big hug and popped downstairs to prepare a three-course meal for eight people and to sew back the rogue wire that had broken loose from her favourite bra.

CHAPTER TWENTY-ONE

This is the best part of the day. Sitting out in the garden, a good day's work behind me, amply rewarded with a welcome soak in a really hot bath. A glass of Irish whiskey nestling in one hand leaving the other free to stroke the tired old tortoiseshell cat that is spreadeagled, flat out, across my knee. An even more dilapidated cat, a white one this time, is stretched out fast asleep across my feet, not having had the strength for such a climb.

Just one slight niggle. I had splashed a dollop of Molton Brown's Heavenly Ginger-lily into the bath – because I'm worth it. But it hadn't bubbled up as I had expected and it slowly dawned on me that I must have picked up the wrong bottle and used their exfoliating toner instead.

Aileen said she thought it would be all right and she generally knows what she's talking about, but as soon as I had a moment to myself I was going to take a quick tour round those hairy bits and pieces that I keep well hidden from public view to see if all was as it should be.

There was a rustle over in the bushes and an anxious black face peered out through the undergrowth. Nokia stalks around the garden as though he's a Japanese soldier who hasn't been told the war is over.

He's losing his puppy fat and the new slim-line Nokia looks even more of a killing machine than ever. But to be absolutely honest, apart from myself on several painful occasions, the postman – one hit and three near misses – and our visiting gardeners Paul and his wife Val, who managed to fend him off with a metal stepladder, he hasn't attacked anyone since his visit to the vet.

Of course I'm not counting the pizza delivery boy who really had it coming to him and if Nokia hadn't sorted him out I would have been in there myself.

A boy racer screamed past the park. Windows rolled right down, radio on at full blast. The driver keeping whatever tune there might have been strictly to himself, leaving me alone with the window-rattling, nerve-jangling, bass beat. I think we should be allowed to hurl half bricks at such cars without fear of prosecution. Hit 'em where it hurts, I say: in their highly polished bodywork.

But today nothing could disturb the air of peace and contentment that had wrapped itself around me. Aileen had another birthday coming up and I didn't have to organize a thing, apart from making sure that on the day there were flowers in every room of the house – which is a hell of a lot of flowers, but involves me only in paying someone whose job it is to see that it's all done properly.

The scent of the flowers would remind Aileen of her special day wherever she went and I could leave all the worrying to Annie and Martyn, who had insisted on taking charge.

I hate organizing any sort of get-together. I love having lots of friends around, but I so desperately want them all to enjoy themselves that I am teetering on the edge of a nervous breakdown all evening. If anyone stops smiling, even for a moment, then I am absolutely sure that it's all been a total disaster. Should a guest tell me that they are having a thoroughly good time I thank them profusely, but deep inside I know that they are just being kind.

Aileen's youngest knows how I feel and has insisted on taking over. She and Martyn are to organize the whole caboodle over the Internet. It's very kind of them. But over the Internet? It's just not natural, is it? I'm sure it will be a total disaster.

Aileen came outside and sat beside me. She had a glass of white wine in her hand.

'What am I drinking?'
'Where did you find it?'

'In the fridge door.'

'Right hand or left hand side?'

'As you look at it?'

'Yes.'

'When it's open?'

'Yes.'

'Left hand.'

'It's a cheap one I'm using for cooking.'

She took a tentative sip, pulled a face and shuddered. 'Ugh! I think it must be an acquired taste.'

I reached out for her glass. 'I'll go and sort it out for you.'

She took another sip, a larger one this time, rolling the wine around in her mouth. 'Do you know, I think I might be acquiring it.'

'It is very cheap.'

She took a really deep slug, emptied her glass and held it out for me. 'I'll try another one, just to make sure.'

I took the glass. 'Has anyone ever told you that you're an absolute pain in the neck?'

She was shocked. Apparently no one ever had.

'I'll have you know that I'm a delight to have around. Everyone says so.'

Nokia, half hidden on the rockery, watched as I took Aileen's glass and tried to shuffle Tigger's boneless body up off my knees and onto the garden table without waking her.

322

She needs her beauty sleep.

Her head hung down over my arm as though her neck had recently been broken and her back legs were spread out over my other arm in anything but a ladylike fashion. Aileen suddenly remembered something.

'I left the hall door open. Tigger was purring her head off on the front step and I didn't want to frighten her.'

I laid Tigger's head carefully down on the table. Perhaps she was having an out-of-body experience. There certainly didn't appear to be anyone in there at the moment.

'When was that?'

'Just before I came out.'

I plucked a rather limp Thermal from my feet, laid him out across the chair and went to investigate.

Tigger's ghost had disappeared, but then I suppose that's what your average ghost does best. I stuck my head out of the door and looked left and then right and then left again, all of which proved to have been a rather pointless exercise when a young black and white cat crept up on me from behind, leapt high in the air and banged his head against my bum.

I gave him a pat.

'Hello, young man.'

'*Food.*'

'And where have you come from?'

'*F-o-o-o-d.*'

'Haven't seen you around before.'

'*Watch – my – lips.*'

'What are you trying to tell me?'

'*F-o-o-o-o-o-o-o-o-d.*'

'Are you hungry?'

'*Good grief – he's hard work, this one.*'

I went off to the kitchen. He followed me. I opened the fridge. He tried to get inside. I pushed him away and took out a packet of boiled ham. He took its place in the fridge. I hauled him out and tucked him under my arm.

'Right, let's go.'

'*Food.*'

'All in good time.'

I wasn't about to take on any more cats. I had to be strong. I led him out through the front gate and up the lane, and then settled him down by the garage door. I wasn't going to make the mistake of feeding him on the premises. He would never leave me alone.

'*Food.*'

'Shut up.'

I could afford to give him the boiled ham because this was going to be the first and very last time I ever fed him. Maybe he had a good home nearby? More likely he didn't. There was no doubt he was very hungry, but I had promised myself – no more cats.

He wolfed it down.

'*More.*'

I gave him what was left of the ham and made a run for it. He was still mopping up the last few bits and pieces as I closed the front door behind me, took a deep breath and felt thoroughly ashamed of myself.

Over the next week or so I put in a lot of time on the book. I had just over sixty thousand words trapped inside the computer, all topped and tailed and ready for public consumption, but I was having great difficulty in going for the final push.

I would write a thousand words in a day, go to bed absolutely chuffed and then edit them down first thing next morning and find that I now had reached the magnificent total of fifty-nine thousand, eight hundred and forty-three.

It's a stage that most writers must go through, but in my case what made it even more depressing was the little document information panel that kept popping up in the top right hand corner of the computer screen. It informed me, rather sarcastically I thought, that the average length of my words throughout the whole manuscript worked out at a miserable four letters. I like to think it was having me on, but I doubt it.

In the meantime life goes on as usual and there are obligations that refuse to go away, but now with an added dimension. First thing every morning I try to concentrate on what has become my daily routine. Shower, clean teeth, get dressed, go downstairs, don't look out of the window.

Pot of coffee on the go, bread in toaster, feed Tigger and Thermal down in the cellar, don't look out of the window.

Place a bowl of Iams out in the back porch for Nokia, prepare breakfast for Aileen and sort out what we are having for dinner tonight. Take cup of coffee up to office, switch on the computer, and – oh, you daft devil, you've gone and looked out of the window.

And there, sitting very still on the other side of the lane from where he has a clear view of our front door and windows, is a hungry young black and white cat who has made it his mission in life to stalk us. If he ever finds out that we have another door round at the back, we're done for.

For once in my life, however, I am determined to stick to my guns. I am definitely not going to feed him. Eventually he'll realize he's on a loser with me and move on. He's a friendly little fellow, with bags of energy and a loving personality. He's a winner. He'll find someone who will take him in. Someone younger than me who is more likely to live as long as he does and give him a good home.

It's just that Sainsbury's had a special offer on Bernard Matthews's boiled ham last

Saturday – buy three packs and get one free – and it seemed a pity not to take advantage of it. I bought six packs, but as soon as that's gone I'm going to be really firm with him.

After he's had his breakfast he has a refreshing nap under the hedge and then, as soon as the shops are open, he sidles off to hang about with his mates up in Marsh, collect his benefits from the post office or whatever it is that he gets up to when he's not hounding me. ⊣

I had now spent the last ten days in iso-lation. The book had inched a few thousand words further on, but I really do need to get out and about and in amongst other people to keep the juices flowing.

Today was going to be different. In the morning, over to Yorkshire Television in Leeds. In the afternoon Halifax, to hear the specialist's verdict on my eye.

I arrived early at the studios and made for the canteen to while away the time with a copy of *Private Eye* and a cup of coffee. Then, as I turned right past reception and made my way down the corridor, I ran straight into Elvis Presley.

'Sorry.'

'Hey, man, no worries.'

This was the older Elvis, the one who had eaten all the pies and put on a pound or two. He turned off into an anteroom on his way to the recording studios.

The door was one of those that take their time when it comes to closing that final inch and I listened in as he warmed up. He was quite remarkable. The original Elvis would have been gobsmacked.

It must have been some sort of a competition. In the canteen there were at least seven other Elvises, all dressed up to the nines and looking the part, but each of them seated at a separate table with his friends and hangers-on.

Wouldn't you have thought that they would have looked upon this as a golden opportunity to mix and match?

'I love your sideburns.'

'Army and Navy Stores, three ninety-nine.'

But no – it was as though the others didn't even exist. After a while a girl brought my Elvis back and took another one away. My Elvis also plonked himself down at a table on his own and stared into space.

As I passed him on my way out I stopped and told him that I thought his singing voice was spot on. He answered in another voice, the one that he'd brought with him all the way up from the West Midlands.

'Well, that's very kind of yo'. I've worshipped that man for every one of my thirty-eight years.'

In an instant the spell was broken and I was just listening to a fat man from Birmingham who had gone and got himself dressed up as Elvis Presley.

Over at the hospital in Halifax the waiting area was absolutely packed. I settled myself down for a long wait and wished I hadn't left my copy of *Private Eye* over in Leeds.

As it turned out the staff did us proud. They whipped us in and out at a rate of knots. However, there was time for the five of us on my row and the five sitting on the row opposite to hold a round table discussion on the pressing matters of the day.

The man sitting next to me said it was all in order because we had a quorum and this was accepted by the rest of us because he'd been in Rotary for over twenty-five years and knew what he was talking about.

The first item on the agenda was to try to work out what the woman who had just gone in to see the doctor had been talking about earlier.

She had high blood pressure, she said. 'I have to take a reversible aspirin first thing every morning.'

Not one of us had the slightest idea what a reversible aspirin might be, not even the man from Rotary, but we managed to co-opt a passing nurse and she suggested that the woman might have meant a dispersible aspirin. We all went along with that.

We then each of us outlined our own particular problems. My map of Wales that had eventually slimmed itself down to the Isle of Wight went down rather well, I thought, only to be topped by a very old man who said nothing at all as he calmly took out his glass eye, wrapped it in a tissue, popped it in his top pocket and replaced his patch.

By the time my name was called I was thoroughly enjoying myself and firing on all cylinders, but the specialist soon put a stop to that.

'Do you realize how lucky you have been?'

He spelt out once more how the lump of cholesterol that had broken away from a vein and finished up in my eye could just as easily have landed up in my brain or in my heart.

'You could have had a stroke or a heart attack.'

I knew that.

'As for your Isle of Wight, I am afraid it will never go away. It will stay with you always. I did consider contacting the DVLA to stop you driving.'

Now I didn't know that.

'At the moment you are very much a borderline case. I will see you again in another six months.'

There was a time in moments of stress when I would catch myself inadvertently talking to myself and feel rather foolish if anyone happened to notice. But nowadays I tend not to bother. At least the two of us are more likely to be on the same wavelength than we would be talking things over with a complete stranger.

Today we drove out of the car park together in a state of shock and it wasn't until we were approaching the Elland bypass that the silence was broken.

'It never even occurred to me.'

'No, well, it wouldn't, would it? That's your trouble – you just don't think.'

'Imagine – not being able to drive.'

'Nightmare.'

'What about Aileen?'

'What about me?'

'She needs me to ferry her about.'

'I haven't been on a bus for over thirty years.'

'It doesn't bear thinking about.'

'Traffic lights ahead.'

'Don't start that – it's not clever.'

The black and white cat was waiting to mug me as I turned the car into the lane. Aileen has started calling him Cosmo for some reason or other. I've warned her that once you do that you are heading for trouble, but she won't have it.

I pressed the little buzzer thingy in the car. The one that asks the automatic garage door if it would kindly mind opening, and it immediately complied. I have no idea how the two of them manage to arrange this little miracle, but they seem only too eager to please and always with a smile. I am most impressed.

So was young Cosmo – you see, I'm doing it now. He ran ahead of me and sat down right in the middle of the garage and waited. I edged the car closer and closer until he disappeared from view below the line of the bonnet. I eased even closer until I must have been almost on top of him, but in the end I had to get out of the car and shift him by hand. I could almost hear the little buzzer thingy in the car complaining.

'I don't know why I bother.'

Cosmo followed me in through the gate and up the path, telling me all about this and all about that.

'For goodness' sake shut up.'

But he can't. It's not in his nature. He just goes on and on, unless he happens to be eating. That, of course, is a different matter altogether and demands his full attention.

As we passed under the wrought iron arch and moved on into the courtyard his purring changed down a gear or two and took on a more thoughtful quality. He looked about him in wonder.

'Why wasn't I told about this?'

He jumped up on a sleeper and began to rummage around in the undergrowth.

'Now I could live here.'

He came across the fountain and stood and stared in wonder.

'Wow! Running water.'

He jumped down and almost landed on top of Nokia.

'Oh, bugger.'

The evil one didn't even see him. A few seconds ago he had been fully occupied in laundering his underbelly. One back leg stuck high in the air, the other wrapped around the back of his neck, head buried deep in his stomach, he looked something like a tepee that had once belonged to a very small Red Indian.

'Where are you, Nokey?'

I hadn't noticed Aileen, but as her gentle tones rolled out from behind the stone steps I saw that Nokia was listening intently.

She was sitting at the garden table. I could just see the top of her head.

'Are you coming to say hello?'

Nokia seemed to be transfixed. He sat and stared at her, his legs still all over the place.

'Come on now, there's my little love.'

She could have had no idea where he was, or if he was there at all, but I wasn't about to interfere. Something different was going on and I wanted to see how it turned out. Nokia rearranged his legs into some sort of order and moved in a little closer. I looked round for Cosmo, but he had made his excuses and left.

I have no idea how long I stood there, not daring to move in case I broke the spell she was weaving.

'Nokey?'

He edged a little closer.

'Come on, boy.'

By this time he was crouching only a couple of feet away from her and I was beginning to feel uncomfortable about letting him get in so close. So was Nokia and he retreated a little way to think this thing through.

It was his body language that made me keep quiet. He looked so vulnerable. It seemed as though he longed desperately to be a part of all this but had absolutely no idea of how to go about it.

'Nokey.'

At the sound of Aileen's voice he stretched long and low. Front end scraping the ground, back end stuck high in the air, front claws reaching out like pitchforks.

'Are you there, Nokey?'

He made a move. At first I thought he would see me, but then he turned off left and slowly made his way up the stone steps. He crouched on the fifth step, on a level with the back of Aileen's head.

Too close, I thought, and began to move forward.

So did Nokia. He reached out, and, with his claws safely tucked out of the way, gently touched her on the shoulder.

'Nokey – is that you?'

He reached out and touched her again.

'Who's a lovely boy?'

Nokia was, apparently, and maybe for the first time in his life he purred. The sound was at first both rusty and short-lived, and it seemed to surprise him as much as it delighted Aileen.

She turned and tried to focus on him.

He backed off, but only for an inch or so.

'Good boy, Nokey.'

He purred very quietly. He was getting the hang of this, but he had no intention of pushing his luck.

The two had eyes only for each other, one softly whispering a series of sweet nothings, the other responding with a gentle murmur of a purr.

And so, like Cosmo, I made my excuses and left.

CHAPTER TWENTY-TWO

I ordered the flowers for Aileen's birthday party by picking up the phone, dialling a florist in Huddersfield town centre and asking her if she could deliver them for me on the date in question. She said she would be only too pleased and I said I would pay her for them on delivery She said that would be fine by her and that is about as complicated as life ever becomes in my little world.

In the meantime those weird things they call e-mails were winging their way out of London to specific targets all over the British Isles and in no time Annie had built herself a firm guest list of her mother's nearest and dearest.

Fortunately Aileen understands how to persuade her computer to part with all this stuff and she would print out the e-mails for me on real paper so that, apart from the daft spelling and the lack of punctuation, they almost looked like proper letters.

At least I have a soulmate in the Tuesday Club. That night we were meeting at Mike and Jean's house. There were only the four of us, Gillian and Martin being otherwise engaged whilst Paul and Alison were over in Romania sorting out a delivery of washing machines on behalf of their charity, Acorn.

Unlike me Mike doesn't quite date back to the Middle Ages and is very much at home with the computer; in fact his business wouldn't be able to function without a whole bank of them. It's all those blessed spin-offs he can't be doing with.

Halfway through the meal he received a text message from Alison.

Tell jean gg sends his love. He's still working hard 4 his old dears. Hope to have solved w/machine probs by 2 morrow.

Mike texted back.

OK.

Within minutes he had a reply.

Is that all U can manage U miserable bastard. What a long and meaningful reply.

We had started and finished off the pudding and were well into the coffee before he finally managed to wrap his fingers round the reply.

Yup. Don't do text.

Bless him.

My daughter Sally arrived a couple of days early for the party, accompanied by an elegant young woman who claimed to be my granddaughter. I had my doubts.

The rear seats of my treasured XJS amount to little more than a narrow leather shelf, but I had always been able to fold little Katie in such a manner that her legs finished up more or less where they would have been had I been the owner of a proper car. This young woman's legs were so long they were all over the place and I swore to myself that I would keep a close eye on her until I discovered who she really was.

Annie and Martyn were the next to arrive. Their car drew up outside the house and a case of champagne got out. It waited patiently on the pavement as several of its mates climbed out through the windows and stacked themselves up by its side, allowing the driver and his lovely wife a few spare inches to tunnel their way out through the passenger door.

It takes a long time to separate Aileen from her children – she is one of the great cuddlers of our time – but after what seemed like an hour or so I grabbed her as she was coming up for air and whisked her off to Trudy's to be shampooed and set.

Over the next twenty-four hours the entire family reported for duty, all except for Sally's Steve that is. Once again the police force had insisted that he stay behind to make sure the streets of Brighton remained safe for decent people to do whatever it is that decent people tend to do on the streets of Brighton.

I missed him. He has green fingers and usually repots all the house plants whilst he's up here. They had been asking when he was coming.

'I'm feeling all hemmed in.'

'I know what you mean. I'm becoming claustrophobic, me.'

Now I would have to tell them that he wasn't coming after all and they would have to wait a while longer. I dreaded the thought. I seem to have been saddled with a load of pot plants that could sulk for England.

As the kids arrived they had each in turn been welcomed on the front doorstep by a small and rather over-excited black and white cat.

'Who's a lovely boy, then?'

'Food.'

'Aren't you a little sweetie?'

'Food.'

He didn't have much luck with Aileen's two sons, David and Paul. They have both inherited their mother's chronic sight problem and in their dark world small cats just don't exist. Had Cosmo been a muscular young donkey wearing a reflective vest and a miner's helmet complete with Davy lamp then he might just have stood an outside chance, but I wouldn't have bet on it.

He ran down the path, straight towards Paul.

'Food.'

Fortunately Paul's wife Wendy is blessed with second sight; it comes with the job. She deflected Cosmo with the merest flick of a petite size four and a half, just as he was about to commit suicide by hurling himself under an oncoming size nine.

He was a little more wary from that moment on and Lubka was able to steer David round him without too much trouble. I have fond memories of her guiding her new husband round the castle in Bratislava just after their wedding.

'It's two steps upski and then three steps downski.'

English as she is spoke.

My daughter-in-law Lisa first laid eyes on Cosmo as he lay stretched out half asleep on the front doorstep. The look on her face would have convinced even the most heartless of cynics that there is definitely such a thing as love at first sight.

She ran and sat on the step beside him.

'Aren't you beautiful?'

He stretched and agreed with her wholeheartedly.

'Mmmmm.'

'You're gorgeous.'

She stroked his cheeks, then ran her fingernails down the full length of his spine, at the same time caressing him with soft and gentle words that folded themselves neatly round him until he seemed to have been switched on to automatic.

'*Mmmmm.*'

At that moment he discovered that there just might be a little more to life than food.

'*Mmmmmmmmmmmmm.*'

Nick watched in silence as the two of them made mad passionate love, right there on the front doorstep. He knew straight away that this wasn't going to be a mere one night stand. It was the first time he had ever laid eyes on Cosmo, but he could read Lisa like a book.

As usual all fourteen of us finished up in the kitchen. Fifteen if you count Alison and it would be a very brave man who didn't count Alison. She was building an arc of balloons out in the hall, but her voice seemed to be right here with us in the kitchen. It gets everywhere. At one point I think it went and nicked something out of the fridge when no one was looking, but I can't be absolutely sure about that.

Before long we were all back out in the hall, partly due to Alison's magnetic personality and partly due to the front door bell. Aileen's eldest Helen had arrived with her young son Luke and the family was complete.

Over the next twenty-four hours I became

very proud of our four young grandchildren. Paul's Grace and Hanna had met before – they happen to be sisters and they live together and it does help – but they had to start from scratch with Luke and Katie. Luke, who had begun life out in the Arab Emirates, had never met any of the girls before and it was also a first time all round for Katie.

After a few brief and slightly awkward introductions they were off, all of them on the same wavelength and having a whale of a time as they embarked on a party all of their own.

Yesterday, long before our widespread tribe had set out on their latest pilgrimage to Huddersfield, I had taken Thermal and Tigger, their sheepskin rugs, their personal radiators and a wide selection of their various toys down to the garden cellar where they would be able to keep themselves to themselves for the next couple of days.

Now I sat on the floor between them and practised the little-known art of cross-legged ambidextrous stroking as they purred softly and tuned their ears in to the unaccustomed stream of noise coming from the kitchen above their heads.

It had been lovely watching the kids as they piled in two by two from all over the place. It was great having them all here, laughing and pitching in together like this, and it would be an especially wonderful moment when Aileen and I waved a tearful goodbye to the lot of them as they all pushed off on Sunday afternoon. When you get to our age you can have too much of a good thing.

Tigger seemed to read my mind and drifted over to her water bowl.

'I'll drink to that.'

Thermal decided not to drink to that. He'd weighed it up. His water bowl was at least a couple of feet away and then of course there was the long journey back to his rug. He settled himself down. He'd wait until it was absolutely necessary

I stroked his head and moved his bowl so that he didn't have to move at all.

We are none of us getting any younger.

As I was taking care of the OAPs down in the cellar, Aileen had left the kids to themselves for a few moments and gone out into the courtyard to have a word with Nokia.

To the casual observer the affair between the two of them wouldn't seem to have progressed all that far, but to those of us who were keeping a close eye on the situation the signs were promising.

This is the way it goes. Aileen sits on her bench and begins talking gently to him. She has no idea whether he is there or not and more often than not he isn't. The odds are

343

that he will be fast asleep in his den; it's what he does best. But Aileen will persist and after a while her soft and gentle voice will work its way through the thick stone walls and Nokia will appear at his front door and look stupid. After even the shortest of naps he's hardly at his best.

Once he has pulled himself together he moves closer and closer towards the voice, until he is maybe a couple of feet away from the bench. He settles himself down and listens intently to what the voice has to say. He seems to know that this moment is especially for him.

After a while he moves in even closer, until he's perhaps less than a foot away, and his cautious body will relax down onto the stone pavers as he is soothed by the gentle tones, which appear to carry no threat whatsoever.

Not until that voice makes the slightest move, that is. Then his black back arches and his claws come out. The claws are on automatic and have no choice in the matter.

The moment the voice stands up he is off like a shot, back behind the thick stone walls of his little den. As I said, the signs are promising. It's just that it could take another twenty years or so.

As everyone disappeared behind a variety of doors to change into something loose and make the best of themselves, Martyn tried his hardest to find something somewhere in the house that would play a compact disc he and Annie had gone to a lot of trouble to prepare especially for the occasion.

He found a thingy and a set of speakers tucked away somewhere on the top floor and carried them down three flights of stairs before he discovered that they didn't work.

Then he hauled something or other up from the basement that he thought might do the trick. It didn't. Then he found something else that looked quite promising at first, but wasn't. I kept out of the way and hoped he wouldn't ask me anything about tweeters and woofers and thank goodness he didn't.

Eventually he had to call it a day because the other guests had begun to arrive and he had appointed himself as wine waiter for the evening.

Cosmo had taken on the job of commissionaire extraordinaire and remained at his post on the front doorstep, meeting and greeting every arrival in his own inimitable style.

'Hello, puss!'

'Food.'

The Tuesday Club arrived en masse, all scrubbed up and bearing gifts. Gillian had made Aileen an enormous chocolate birthday cake that had experienced something of a nervous breakdown as she'd taken it out of the oven.

Gillian's cakes are not allowed to be anything but perfect but she needn't have worried. This one tasted wonderful. It just wobbled a lot and burst into tears if you shouted at it.

Cosmo got a larger than life greeting from Mary Wibberley, the larger than life romantic novelist and queen of Mills & Boon romances.

'*Food.*'

'You just stay there.'

He did as he was told.

You tend to do that if Mary tells you to.

After giving Aileen a quick kiss she dived in under a tablecloth that covered a vast selection of cold meats, fish and salads and then disappeared back outside to present Cosmo with a plate full of goodies the like of which he had never seen before in his whole short life. After a tentative start he really tucked in and wolfed down everything Mary had laid before him with the sole exception of the pickled cucumber.

Job done, she then set up a smokers only table in the kitchen with her friend Jenny, fellow author Marion Hough, the Tuesday Club's Jean and our old friend Bridie from across the back lane.

Bridie hadn't wanted to intrude.

'Now I'm not staying long, I'll just have the one wee drink with you and then I'll be on my way.'

Several hours later she repeated the statement as she led the community singing from the big settee in the lounge.

Aileen was having a wonderful time. She has the most beautiful smile and it hadn't had a minute to itself all day. Safe on home territory she moved amongst her guests with great confidence and they in turn shimmied and swayed out of her way whenever it looked as though she might separate them from their glass of wine or their virginity or whatever.

'Where's Mary Wib?'

'She's in the kitchen.'

She had been, but she wasn't now. And then she was. She came striding back in through the porch door and looked guilty as she caught sight of us.

'There was a cat sitting out in the porch and so I gave him a few scraps.'

'You didn't touch him?'

'He wouldn't let me.'

'Best not – it hurts.'

I put my head round the door to see if it really was Nokia that Mary had tried to feed, but all I could see was a tuft of black fur sticking up over the top of the small mountain of beef, chicken, pork, ham and salmon she had piled high on a dinner plate for him.

He reversed a little so that he could focus

on this enormous mound of whatever it was, then sat down and tried to work out what on earth he was supposed to do with it.

'He only ever has those biscuity things from Iams.' I bent to remove the dish and his claws reached out towards me. 'But I'll leave it with him for the moment – just in case.'

A little while later Aileen and I were at the kitchen table, knocking back the odd glass of wine and attempting to persuade the swirling cigarette smoke to come over here and sit with us, when a black furry head poked itself round the foot of the open door.

At first it seemed somewhat smaller than the black furry head that ran wild out in the courtyard, but I think that must have been nerves. It backed off into the porch for a moment or so to think this through and then popped itself round the door once more and settled down to watch the goings-on.

He had never done that before. He had shown absolutely no interest whatsoever in whatever it was that went on in here, but now his whiskers positively thrummed as they took in the noise, the many bodies and the red carpet in the dining area.

Especially the red carpet. He couldn't take his eyes off it. He was hardly likely to have come across anything quite like it before and he eased himself a little further in through the door to get a closer look.

'*Wow!*'

He inched a little closer.

'*When I grow up I'm going to have one of those.*'

This was the very first time since the early days that I had thought of him as a young cat. He had always seemed older than his years. Never played, never been enthusiastic about anything, but now his body language was alive and living in our kitchen.

I was the only one who had spotted him so far and I kept the news to myself because I didn't want him frightened off. I wanted to see where he would go from here and I supposed the answer to that would be halfway up the wall.

A miserable excuse for a breeze appeared out of nowhere and gently closed the kichen door behind him. Nokia was only aware of what was happening at the very last minute and by then it was too late.

He simply froze and stared at the door. I left the table and went over to open it for him. He saw me coming and panicked, racing out of the kitchen and into the hall.

The hall was an absolute jungle of legs, but he was desperate and decided to go for it, weaving his way in and out of them at high speed until he thought he saw a glimpse of the outside world through yet another damn forest, this time made up of a bunch of much younger legs.

The kids nearly dropped their sparklers as a solid ball of black fur rattled in and out of their ankles and shot towards the front door. There was one further obstruction in his way. A small black and white cat was being seduced by a beautiful young woman on the front step. Nokia didn't even adjust his stride. He clambered right over the top of the reclining Cosmo's torso and disappeared out into the dark night.

By the time I arrived on the scene of the crime Cosmo was in a state of shock and looked as though he might not be long for this world. I bent to listen to his last words.

'Food.'

On the other hand we might just be able to save him. I worked my way back through the crowded hall and into the kitchen. I knew where we had food to spare. I checked my watch. Cosmo hadn't eaten for almost three-quarters of an hour. Any further delay could be fatal.

I collected the dish Mary had put out in the back porch and Lisa gradually brought him back from the brink by sitting him on her knee and feeding it to him by hand.

I left them to it and ventured out into the darkness to see if I could find young Nokia. The night didn't stay dark for very long as sensor after sensor switched on light after light, but there was no sign at all of a disturbed black cat.

A mangy old ginger tom sat having a drink from the pond.

'Could you spare us a bite to eat, sor?'

'Try the lady at the front door.'

'Ah, God bless you, sor.'

But I couldn't see Nokia. He would be hiding out there, watching me from behind something or other, and I wondered where I had gone wrong. Of all the cats that had come into my life over the years he was the only one who had decided that I wasn't to be trusted.

I parked myself down on Aileen's bench and called out his name but to no avail and it was then that I made up my mind. One way or another I was going to win him over.

But I didn't.

Aileen did.

TAILPIECE

I had stripped all the beds and piled the sheets and pillow cases out on the landing. I added a bundle of towels to the pile and was just about to separate my whites from my coloureds when the phone burst into life. It was Nick ringing from Stratford.

'Hi, Dad – is Cosmo still with you?'

'He's having a nap under the hedge at the moment. Can I give him a message?'

'Will he be with you for the next couple of hours or so?'

'Should be. Why?'

'Lisa's decided. We're coming to get him.'

Cosmo was absolutely delighted to see them. He met them at the gate and ran happily in front of them all the way up the path. He rubbed his head against Lisa's leg as she told me what they had in store for him. They had called in to see a vet before they started out this morning. He had agreed to separate Cosmo from his testicles this very afternoon, give him all the necessary jabs and place an identity chip in his neck.

'And then you're coming home to live with us, aren't you, Cosmo?'

The little cat rolled over onto his back, sighed contentedly and gave a great big stretch. You can make a real fool of yourself if you don't speak the language.

It wasn't until Nick produced the wire cage and set it down on the porch floor that certain doubts began to creep into Cosmo's mind. After a short and playful skirmish between two rather decent chaps, man's hand pushing at cat's bum, cat's claws digging deep into doormat, what had started out as a mere battle of wills turned into all-out war.

Cat's claws embedded in man's arm – man holds cat in air by scruff of neck – blood pours from man's arm – cat gets thump on bottom – cat bites man's thumb – cat gets another thump on bottom – cage stood up on end – cat dropped into cage from great height – cage doors slammed shut and door locked – cat works out combination of lock and escapes.

It seemed to go on for ever. I produced a set of elbow-length gardening gloves from down in the cellar, thought about it for a moment or two and then decided that Nick's need was marginally greater than Cosmo's.

Eventually the small but noble savage had to admit defeat, although he continued with his protests at the top of his voice. He was absolutely furious, and informed them in no uncertain terms that his solicitors would be getting in touch.

'Would you like a cup of coffee?'

'Thanks, Dad, but we'd better be off.'

Apparently the tirade continued at full blast as they passed the outskirts of Derby, and carried on intermittently as Lichfield faded into the distance, but then it seemed that he had accepted his fate and run out of steam.

Maybe he was simply stunned into silence by the conversation that was being conducted by his two adversaries up front.

He had left Huddersfield as Cosmo the cat. Fifty miles on his name was officially declared to be Archie. Twenty miles further down the road it was changed by deed poll and he became Freddie.

They were closing in on Stratford and his new home when Lisa finally declared that from now on he would be known to the entire world as Harvey Longden.

So Harvey it is and he rather likes it; it's grown on him. He lives surrounded by fields, not a stone's throw away from Anne Hathaway's cottage, where he hunts and fishes from morning to night and then goes home to a cooked meal and a great big cuddle from two special people who love him to bits.

Not bad for a young lad who started out on the streets of Huddersfield, going round, door to door, begging for *'Foood!'*

Meanwhile back at the ranch Nokia was still playing hard to get. For some reason he seemed to feel quite safe stretched out in the courtyard, not a couple of feet away from the two of us, listening in as I read the newspaper out loud to Aileen. He always perked up during the show business gossip but then quietly slipped into a coma the moment I started on the sport. I blame Aileen for setting him a bad example.

He never made a sound. Not a purr, not a hiss or a sigh – nothing – but his body language spoke volumes. It was forever on guard, suspecting the worst. And yet there were moments when you could feel that inside he was aching for something about which he knew nothing – something a bit better than this.

He would eat his meals in the back porch, have a right good fettle and then settle down on the doormat to watch the world go by, while Aileen held a one-way conversation with him through the open door as she washed up and piled the pots and pans in a haphazard stack on the draining board.

After she had disappeared up to her office I continued the conversation as I stuck the lot back in the sink and washed them properly. She's a trier, bless her, but there are times when it's not enough.

He would listen to every word we had to

say, but the moment we moved a little closer he was off like a shot, out into the night.

The breakthrough came one evening as the sun decided to play silly devils and we had to shift the garden table and chairs in order to stay with it. This left a much narrower gap than usual between Aileen's chair and the wooden sleepers that fold themselves neatly round the flower beds.

Nokia had to pass very close to Aileen's chair that evening as he came out of his hut to join us, and her hand happened to be hanging down loose from the arm rest. As he strolled by, her fingers inadvertently brushed down the length of his spine and up against the base of his tail.

Startled, she yanked them away just as Nokia swung round to deal with whatever it was that had so rudely interfered with his person.

Then he sat down, had a damn good lick and thought about it. Actually, it hadn't been all that unpleasant. Rather nice, in fact. What he might do was stroll casually back in the other direction and see what happened. Now Aileen's eyes can't really make him out, but a big black blur passing slowly by her ankle does rather stand out against the pale stone pavers. She tensed herself, somewhat worried about coming into contact with the end that contains all the teeth, and waited until the first portion of the blur had passed her by before once more trailing her fingers down the length of his spine. Had he been reversing she would have found herself in a whole lot of trouble.

He must have paced back and forth by her chair a dozen times, each time a little slower than the last as Aileen soothed his nerves with her smooth, silky voice and he allowed her fingers to linger that little bit longer and deeper in the fur along his black velvet back.

He would sit down, have yet another good lick and think about it, then off he would go again.

'He's coming, Aileen.'

Eventually he took a break, lying flat out a foot or so away from Aileen's chair.

Every so often he would yawn and stretch out to his full length, each time his body finishing up a little closer to Aileen's foot. She continued to chat away softly to him and then, as he stretched out for what probably was a personal best, his front paw reached out and brushed against the toe of her sandal.

He jumped back as though scalded. Aileen simply carried on talking to him as though nothing had happened and after a while he settled back down and put on yet another Olympic display of yawning and stretching until his paw came to rest on her foot once more.

This time he left it there and pretended to drop off to sleep.

Later that night I was busy cremating a couple of bacon rashers which were about to join a matching pair of over-fried eggs in a couple of seeded brown baps and Aileen was at the kitchen table, knocking back a gin and tonic in a vain attempt to anaesthetize her taste buds, when a wary black face peered round the foot of the door.

'Hi, Nokey.'

The coast was clear. Thermal and Tigger had finished their supper just a few minutes ago. I had taken them back downstairs and tucked them in. They had managed to grab barely ten hours' sleep since breakfast and were absolutely shattered.

Nokia kept a close eye on me as I served up my burnt offering and then relaxed somewhat as I took my place at the table. Leaving the safety of the door behind him he first sidled up against the sink unit and then eased his way a little further in until he was sitting on that tile just behind Aileen's chair, the one with the old cigarette burn that I'm going to do something about one of these days. It looked so much better with a cat's bottom sitting on it, but no sooner had he eased his rear end into place than he caught sight of his new friend the red carpet.

It seemed to hypnotize him.

'Look into my eyes.'

The carpet crooked its little finger and beckoned him over. Like a sleepwalker he answered the call, sinking down into the rich red pile and pounding and pounding with pure pleasure until a wave of ecstasy swept down the length of his body. Then he tidied his legs away underneath himself and began to purr.

It was one hell of a purr. I couldn't decide whether it reminded me of an old Massey Ferguson tractor ticking over on a cobbled farmyard somewhere in Devon or a Lancaster bomber on its way back from Dresden.

'What on earth is that?'

'It's Nokey.'

'Good grief.'

If it startled the pair of us, it frightened the life out of Nokia. He couldn't work out where on earth it was coming from. At first he seemed to think he must have a leak somewhere, but after a close examination of his underbelly and his private parts he decided that it had nothing to do with him whatsoever and settled down on the carpet once again.

He purred on for the next couple of hours or so, by which time he seemed to be getting the hang of it. Though just as loud, it had taken on a more musical quality that resonated with sheer happiness, especially whenever Aileen came close and chatted to him. A year since he arrived and never a sound

359

out of him, and now we couldn't shut him up.

Midnight came and went and eventually I had to ask him to leave. I wasn't at all prepared for this moment. I thought we would never win him over.

He shot out of the back door like a rabbit, then once out in the courtyard he turned and gave me the most heart-rending look.

'I knew it was too good to last.'

Then, head slumped on his chest, he walked miserably over to his little home under the stone steps. For a moment I thought about cutting off a piece of the dining room carpet for him as a comfort blanket.

By the weekend I'd fitted a brand new cat flap down in the cellar and bought him a fancy new bed. The pet shop assured me that this was absolutely the latest thing in cat accessories, fashioned as it was in a rather fetching brown suede. I bought it for him because it was about the size of a skip.

I found an extra large litter tray on Huddersfield market and decided to switch back to non-clumping cat litter. The clumping variety is designed to absorb every last drop of liquid and had long been threatening me with a hernia whenever I cleared it out. The amount of cat litter in Nokia's tray would just about finish me off.

Now for the moment of truth. Was he

ready for all this? Over the past few days he had been waiting on the back step first thing every morning and fallen straight into the porch as I opened the door. He made straight for the carpet and settled down happily. Aileen had even managed a tentative stroke every now and then without losing a single drop of blood.

But we'd had to leave the back door open because he wasn't toilet trained, and keep the hall door shut so that he couldn't roam throughout the house. He wouldn't know how to use the cat flap and how would he cope with the two old-age pensioners who slept in the cellar next door?

It was time to find out. I lured him down the outside cellar steps with his saucer of Iams. Once down there I plonked it on a shelf above the door, knelt down and pointed to the saucer I'd planted earlier on the other side of the cat flap. He stared at it in amazement.

'*How the hell did he do that?*'

With more than a little trepidation I put my head down close to his and pushed the little window to and fro with my hand.

'Now what you do, Nokey, is...'

He didn't bother waiting to hear what I had to say. He leapt straight in through the cat flap and began to tuck into his supper.

I couldn't believe it. How did he know? I followed him in – through the door, not the

361

cat flap – and waited to see what he would do next. Once he had finished off the Iams he went straight over to the litter tray, sat down, had a rather serious dump and covered it expertly with a couple of comprehensive flicks of the paw. Then he set off on a tour of the premises.

The carpet shop up in Marsh had been clearing out sample carpet squares, five for a pound. I had bought him a set, stuck one in his outside kennel, placed the red one by the side of his new bed so that he could wipe his feet before retiring for the night and put the other three away in stock.

He had a good look round the back of the boiler and the first thing he saw as he emerged from the other side was the red carpet sample. He was quite overcome.

'Oh, you shouldn't have.'

He raced over and settled down on it, squeezed his huge claws in ecstasy and began to purr like a fire engine.

I made my excuses and left.

Six months have passed and he is a pleasure to have around. He has hardly stopped purring for a minute. He purrs when he's wide awake and often purrs even louder when he's fast asleep. We have to tell him to shut up whenever we answer the phone. He takes not the slightest notice.

'What the hell's that?'

'Sorry. It's the cat.'

'Good grief.'

He is the gentlest of animals. He sits on the back step and purrs as he watches the birds feeding in the garden.

'Look out – there's a cat.'

'Don't worry – it's only Nokes.'

He loves it when we have company, especially the Tuesday Club. He's made friends of them all and makes sure that they are each given an equal ration of his time.

He loves the handsome black cat who lives behind the glass oven door – it's the spitting image of himself and he sits and stares at it for ages. Whenever I open the oven door he runs over to see if it's coming out to play.

And yet playing is what he finds most difficult. He missed out on being a kitten and he doesn't know what to do. He'll chase after a table tennis ball, but once he has it roped and tied he just sits there and looks at it.

He spends most of his time with his beloved Aileen, either sitting up close to her in her office or walking by her side. I do, however, have a single ace up my sleeve. I can click my fingers and Aileen can't. At the sound of my masterful click he comes running over and then walks to heel with me wherever I choose to go.

As long as I stay this side of the garden gate, that is. He absolutely refuses to venture out into the big wide world. He has bad memories of out there and intends to spend the rest of his life in here.

He is nowhere near as adventurous as Thermal was at his age, nor as commanding as Tigger is now. He has very little confidence in himself, hates any kind of trouble and, having skipped the kitten stage, doesn't have the personality of a Cosmo. He simply loves being with people and loves being loved. But most of all he loves being with Aileen.

We have a lot in common.

The publishers hope that this book has given you enjoyable reading. Large Print Books are especially designed to be as easy to see and hold as possible. If you wish a complete list of our books please ask at your local library or write directly to:

Magna Large Print Books
Magna House, Long Preston,
Skipton, North Yorkshire.
BD23 4ND

This Large Print Book, for people
who cannot read normal print,
is published under the auspices of

THE ULVERSCROFT FOUNDATION

... we hope you have enjoyed this book.
Please think for a moment about those
who have worse eyesight than you ...
and are unable to even read or enjoy
Large Print without great difficulty.

You can help them by sending a
donation, large or small, to:

**The Ulverscroft Foundation,
1, The Green, Bradgate Road,
Anstey, Leicestershire, LE7 7FU,
England.**
or request a copy of our brochure for
more details.

The Foundation will use all donations
to assist those people who are visually
impaired and need special attention
with medical research, diagnosis
and treatment.

Thank you very much for your help.